HANYA HOLM

Also by Walter Sorell

BOOKS

The Dance Has Many Faces
The Dance Through the Ages
The Story of the Human Hand

TRANSLATIONS

Arch of Triumph by Erich Maria Remarque
(with Denver Lindley)
Steppenwolf by Hermann Hesse
Goethe's World (anthology)
The Language of Dance by Mary Wigman

PLAY

Everyman Today: A Modern Morality Play

HANYA HOLM

The Biography of an Artist

BY WALTER SORELL

WESLEYAN UNIVERSITY PRESS

Middletown, Connecticut

To Mary Wigman

Contents

List of Illustrations

following page

Acknowledgments

I ACKNOWLEDGE with gratitude my indebtedness to the editors of the Wesleyan University Press as well as to Hanya Holm for entrusting me with the task of writing this book. Miss Holm kindly and patiently talked to me for hours, days, and many weeks and was instrumental in letting me observe her classes at Colorado College in Colorado Springs.

I am indebted to John Martin for letting me quote his writings profusely; to Walter Terry for having spoken to me about Hanya; to Alwin Nikolais and Dr. Juana de Laban, who both dictated several reels of tape for me on their thoughts about and experiences with Hanya; to Mary Wigman for letting me have some of her notes on Hanya; to Valerie Bettis, Don Redlich, Glen Tetley, and to the many students and former coworkers with Hanya for their kindness in sharing their reactions to Hanya with me.

I also wish to say thanks to Mr. K. Wright Dunkley, who taped Hanya's classes in Colorado in 1964 and transcribed her remarks, lectures, and random speeches. I used some of these in the chapter "Hanya Speaks." Furthermore, my thanks go to Marcia B. Siegel for her help and assistance.

W. S.

HANYA HOLM

By Way of Introduction

THERE are many ways of writing a biography, I assume, as many as there are subjects to be written about and writers eager to write about them. But I suspect that in every case there can be only one right way of doing justice to the personality and the biographer.

To choose the approach encompassing everything without spelling it out, leaving enough room for the imagination of the reader to complete the image of the human being, is all that seems to matter. Looking through a magnifying glass, we may be frightened by the many freckles on the face. But the biographer must paint a few characteristic freckles to give the face the humanness it has.

No biography can neglect the environment from which the subject came and into which he grew. Sometimes only a vivid description of the environment will give the personality its three-dimensionality. As in our case, it may be her mirror reflection, giving the image depth beyond the mirror's smooth surface, or it may shape the drama by being her antagonist.

The biographer looks constantly through window panes into interiors. He tries to catch glimpses of the person in moments of unawareness. He sits at her feet and listens to her telling the story. He often plays her voice back on the tape recorder when alone with himself, his writing conscience, and a sheet of white paper. He acts the inquisitive reporter and runs from person to person who has ever been in touch with her. Tell me what do you know about . . . ? What was she like when . . . ? What did she say at the time . . . ? He buries himself in old magazines and records, blowing the dust away to see the past and present as the continuum our life is.

Every answer to his questions is true and yet is colored by personal experience. A hundred answers re-create the multicolored mosaic which the real picture is. There are many truths to our life. There are at least as many truths as there are facets to our being. And yet we are simple in our complexity. We are recognizable through our actions as much as through our faces — even though not everyone sees us the same way.

Then the biographer ought to have a hundred eyes. But, in fact, he only needs one eye, the inner eye that can see the human being's expression that is truly real because it is intangible, the face hidden in its own mystery.

Only on the surface is every man an open book. Begin to leaf through it, and the pages grow in their number and soon defy being numbered at all. It is an exciting adventure to rewrite a book of life, balanced and unbalanced in its many details, with all its credit and debit pages, with its letters of triumph and silent commas of accusations, with its many question marks and marks of exclamation.

One hopes that every reader can sense that this life has been lived, consciously from minute to minute, in full awareness of its meaning so that it also may have meaning to others. The struggle of one life ought to become the message of the book for many.

In the last analysis, the biographer is a scribe who follows the dictate and dictation of a voice stronger than all other voices, including his own. At least this biographer listened attentively to the one voice that is Hanya Holm's.

EARLY YEARS

I never said I wanted to be a choreographer. I am impatient with people who set out to be something without first trying.

— HANYA HOLM

From Convent to Dalcroze

MAINZ on the Rhine is one of the great historical cities of Germany and only recently became an industrial center. Originally Mainz developed around a Roman camp, the Maguntiacum, whose remains have always reminded citizens of the early beginnings of their town. Once it was the seat of archbishops who ruled over considerable territory and, at one time, had the right to crown the Holy Roman Emperor. A mighty cathedral with a beautiful dome has long symbolized the power of the Catholic Church in this city. Johann Gutenberg, the European inventor of the printing press, was born there, lived and worked in Mainz most of his lifetime. And it was in Mainz that Hanya Holm spent the years of her youth, her formative years, before she went to Hellerau to study with Dalcroze and later to Dresden to dance with Mary Wigman.

Hanya was born in Worms, which lies only a few kilometers from Mainz. She was the daughter of Marie (Moerschel) and Valentin Eckert. Her father was a practical man, a wine merchant whose family included some brewers well known in Bavaria. Her mother's family was much more interested in the arts; although there were no great artists among them, they wrote poetry, loved music, and painted. Her mother, vivacious and intellectually curious, was not a typical German *hausfrau*. She was a student of chemistry and became an ardent amateur scientist who had several patented discoveries to her credit.

Hanya still remembers the little room that was turned into

a laboratory. At one time there was a great need for rubber and cork in Germany. Her mother experimented with the idea of an *Ersatz* cork, but this invention was not completed. Her mother died while working on it, during the first World War, in 1917.

"I seem to have inherited the practical side of my ancestors as well as their ability to go off into a world of fantasy, of the impossible," Hanya says. "I certainly inherited my mother's inquisitiveness, the inmost need to find out what hides behind things. This trait of my mother had strongly impressed me when I was still quite young, it must also have left its imprint on my thinking. Because ever since I can remember I have tried to find out whether something could be created or made or found on my way through life."

Hanya spent her first twelve years of schooling at the "Konvent der englischen Fräulein." Her mother had selected this school for her because it had the reputation of being an excellent institute with a record for solid education. What seemed to have been of even greater importance to her mother was the teachers' attitude of taking a very personal interest in each student, an advantage over the more crowded municipal schools. For the teaching at this convent was, for the time, not only very progressive; it was also conducted in small classes permitting a close relationship between student and teacher. After Hanya had graduated, she asked for permission to take postgraduate courses for one more year and, her request granted, she studied with only four or five students in each class as if in a seminar.

Because the school was a convent and thus Church-subsidized, it could afford to delegate its teachers to such small classes. In the main, the teachers were nuns. But several teachers, who taught special courses, came from other schools of higher learning. Hanya fondly remembers a very well-known preacher who taught history at the convent but who could also be heard sermonizing in the cathedral quite often. Although his course was religiously orientated, it adhered to a very fair, worldly, and acceptable viewpoint. In spite of the fact that the school was a Catholic institution, Hanya had among her schoolmates Protestant and also a few Jewish girls. This only proved the reputation of the convent as a school, and Hanya found that each teacher, having his or her personal attraction, knew how to make his subject interesting and alive.

In these formative years Hanya learned, she feels now, a respect for knowledge and creative ability, an understanding of the close interrelation of every branch of knowledge, iron discipline, and a belief in perfection. Where the teaching was insufficient — at least from Hanya's viewpoint and with respect to her later career — was in the discipline of physical education, in the framework of which she learned little more than good manners and deportment, how to sit down, how to greet, how to walk. "I'll never forget how our teacher made us walk, each of us singly, how he crouched on the floor, watching us and shouting from time to time: 'As long as I can see you flopping your soles after you, you walk incorrectly! Don't slur!' His teaching did not go beyond improving the carriage. Well, the room was too small for anything else. So I went once a week to our *Turnverein*, which met in a huge gym with all the necessary equipment. We played all kinds of ball games, particularly during the summer months when we went out into the field. Because of my gymnastic exercises I was physically fit, but in no way ready to perform externalizations of music as was demanded of me when I came to Dalcroze."

The city of Mainz with its many vestiges from Roman days had great meaning in Hanya's growing-up process. Her history and geography lessons closely related to what the children could see around them. The constant sight of the *Römersteine*, stones from the Roman days, and of the *Neue Brunnen*, which was not really new but the old fountain the Romans had built, and of their pile-dwellings of which there were still some to be seen — all this, in its inevitable aesthetic and cultural influence, impressed the artistically inclined young girl a great deal. The vividness and closeness with which the *Nibelungen* saga could be absorbed and compared with Greek and Roman mythology had particular meaning for Hanya then and later. She was told in vivid images about a pagan pageant, the crowning of the Goddess of Reason, which once took place in the same church in which she made her first Communion. In short, she was made aware of the constant flow of history, she grew up with the realization of the past as a part of the present. All these influences laid the foundation for her need and desire "to search, to find out how all this came about and what deeper meaning there was to it." The vision of the majestic cathedral of Mainz never left her, and a remark she made only recently must be understood in the light of these early impressions:

"Architects cannot build churches any more. They build verticals, but not everything that points to the sky has that indivisible life that the old cathdrals have which give you a feeling of elation. The desert can give you a more definite feeling of transport than these modern glass or steel churches, the mountains have better towers than those they now build."

Mainz was a colorful city. It was once occupied by the French, who had left their mark essentially by corrupting the German language spoken in this territory, a daily language which used many Gallic words. The Rhine played a great part in the life of the people. And Hanya says: "When I was young I could never imagine living somewhere else. The river alone was to me like a door that opened into the world, its steady flow was a reminder of life to me, of that life that never stops. Moreover, I learned to swim in the Rhine."

Then there was carnival time in Mainz, and in the days when Hanya was young they were the gayest three days of the year. "When on Saturday the crazy people with Prince Carnival came to town, there was great excitement. From that moment on nobody in town was or wanted to be normal. Those who had no costume to wear turned their jackets inside out. Every horse had a hat on, every dog another whimsical collar. Mainz had its milkmaids at that time who always wore starched triangular head pieces and many skirts. Even they, marked by a fancy uniform, put on something that was even more fanciful. The policemen stood around in the midst of all this wanton gaiety, reminders of an almost forgotten life. Everyone dropped all formalities, there was an all-embracing lightness in the streets and on the public squares. "No," says Hanya, "there was no dance stimulation coming from these festive days. But there was another tremendous stimulation and a lesson to be learned. It was the signal to let go, and if you could not do so when the opportunity was there, if you missed it for whatever reason, then it was too bad for you, that was that, you had had your chance."

Hanya had a very happy home life in her youth. The house where they lived had a large courtyard. There she did her rope-jumping, which she loved, and in winter her father sprayed a big enough section of the yard to make it possible for her to learn ice skating. From her early youth she enjoyed everything connected with physical activity.

As if she had wanted to train her imaginative qualities, she carved and cut and put together her own dollhouse. She had learned carving in school. She took the wood of cigar boxes, which was smooth and did not splinter, and she made tables, chairs, beds, and even the necessary kitchen furniture including a stove. The house was complete with doors and windows and a carpet beater. It was a minute carving job — sometimes a finger was bleeding, but she did not mind. This dollhouse of hers was a living thing of which she did not easily tire. When Hanya no longer liked certain pieces of furniture, she threw them out and carved new ones.

She never played with dolls as most girls do. Playing mother and family, combing the dolls' hair and dressing and undressing them did not satisfy her. But, as though recognizing the seriousness of life, she would sew the clothes for her dolls, the skirts, blouses, and underwear. Again it was an activity she needed, wedding the practical sense to her imagination. She remembers: "There was always some kind of activity by which

I was fascinated, there was always something to do, to be found out. And there was plenty of entertainment. If it wasn't something that existed, I invented it or made it with my own hands."

She began to study the piano privately when she was ten and was introduced to music appreciation at the Hoch Conservatory in Frankfort-am-Main at the age of sixteen. She commuted from Mainz to Frankfort several times a week because the study of music began to mean more and more to her. It was at that period that she also became acquainted with the magic world of the stage, although her parts were little more than walk-ons. But the great stage magician, Max Reinhardt, was the director, and from that time on the stage has never lost its attraction for her. It became the focal point of her life.

After her graduation from the convent she attended the music-oriented Institute of Emile Jaques-Dalcroze — first at Frankfort and later at Hellerau near Dresden — from which, four years later, she was graduated. Her reasons for joining Dalcroze were simple. She had studied rhythm as an extension of her music education and this alone brought her in touch with Dalcroze. But it became more obvious from year to year that she was not the type to sit and practice on a musical instrument for eight or ten hours a day. She needed something to occupy her physically, and it was therefore suggested that she take up music visualization as presented by Dalcroze.

There her ear was thoroughly trained, she took music improvisation on the piano, theory, analysis, composition. But especially Dalcroze demanded that what she learned musically she must also express physically. In other words, she was asked to do improvisations to rhythmic or musical themes. She felt that she could do what was required as well as anyone else, if not better. But here her restlessness and self-criticism made themselves felt: she did not deem satisfactory *what* she did and the way she was supposed to do it. She realized that the musical content could become a physical experience, that there could be a bigger dimension to it. She expected more from her body.

Dissatisfaction led to a new phase in her life. In 1921 when she saw a performance by Mary Wigman in Dresden, she decided then and there that the next step to be taken was to join Wigman. By then Hanya had progressed so far that she was permitted to teach the Dalcroze method, which she did for a while. The main reason why she felt she ought to join Mary Wigman was the need for a physical outlet beyond the mere realization of rhythm. At that time she neither aimed at nor thought of making the dance her career.

The Influence of Mary Wigman

HANYA was married to painter-sculptor Reinhold
Martin Kuntze at the time she met Mary Wigman. They had a
son, but the marriage was soon terminated. Of that situation
she now says, "My decision to dance with Mary Wigman coincided with my divorce. It was to be another kind of marriage
for me, one to last forever. I personally find it difficult to understand that anyone completely dedicated to his art can also fully
devote himself to another person. I don't say it isn't possible,
and I certainly think highly of companionship. But for me, the
slightest attempt to be deterred, physically or by moral obligations, from what I want to do, can throw me off balance."

Mary Wigman tells of an incident shortly after Hanya had
joined her group:

"Once I met her in a streetcar. She held a gaily crying baby
in her lap. 'My son Klaus,' she said with pride when I asked her
who the child was. At that moment I learned to admire Hanya.

"She was very brave; for not only did she have to take care
of herself, she alone had all the responsibilities for her child.
The child's father failed her. Thus, the years of her study were
doubly burdened. She took all this upon herself without any
complaint."

To join Mary Wigman was a logical development in Hanya's
life, not an arbitrary decision. It was the result of her constant
search for the inner experience that brings peace of mind — and
with this gratification, new desires for the excitement of new

experiences. When she saw Mary Wigman dance she was gripped by the wish to find out whether one could acquire the knowledge and skill which led to Wigman's art.

At that time Mary Wigman was fighting her lonely struggle for recognition as a modern dancer. It was the period of expressionism in Germany, the time in which all old values were re-evaluated and the artist searched for new ways of expression. Although the public was rather open-minded and easily accepted every new experimental form, people seemed rather relucant when it came to the dance. Strangely enough, in the mind of most people the dance was still closely assoicated with the classical ballet or with the frothy lightness of the waltz. Everything about it had to be lovely, full of pink and white blossoms. But suddenly there was Mary Wigman with her predominantly dark images of life, with the world of her inmost experiences, with her danced confessions, which bore testimony to her own being and, beyond that, to mankind as reflected in her. But gradually, as Mary Wigman broke down audience resistance, many people began to recognize that there was more to the dance than leg-swinging, kicking, and turning; that there could be a deep emotional expression in it, re-creating the universal drama of the human being as he struggles, fails, and succeeds. Hanya says that finally the bulk of the public came to realize that the modern dance was the equivalent of the dramatic experiments of those days and that Mary Wigman was the Eleonora Duse of the dance.

In the early fifties in her essay, "The Mary Wigman I Know," published in the anthology *The Dance Has Many Faces,* Hanya referred to these first years of Wigman's struggle:

> From the very beginning of her career, every audience has gone through a shock experience which probably was repeated at every performance she gave. It was created by her so definite attitude to the profound and profoundly human problems she dealt with, by her portraits of the eternal struggle of the self with itself and the environment whose product it is. When she came to America in the beginning of the 1930s, she had already

achieved world-wide reputation. But even then the voices of the doubters and deniers were still heard in her own country where it had taken her years of endurance and a strong belief in herself to overcome the opposition of the public and critics alike, ranging from indifference to loud derision.

Hanya says of herself that she was fortunate in having joined Mary Wigman at a time when she and her group were in a stage of discovering what dance meant or would one day mean to them. These were hard-working but happy days for Hanya, who fully enjoyed "this finding out," working with a group under Mary Wigman's guidance. They had to teach themselves and teach one another what they hoped to discover. They learned from Mary to doubt, never to accept anything as final. Mary, who was of course the most advanced of them, gave them the best example: "After each performance, after each new attempt she would call herself to a most private trial where she had to account for every movement. And every time the result was the same — a qualified sentence: Not yet strong enough, to begin once more from the beginning."

The group became accustomed to probe and to query, and the questions were those which each artist must ask himself. Hanya refers to these questions as the greatest impersonal taskmasters and explains that the members of the group all had to participate actively in the creation of a dance, instead of lending their bodies and personalties to be shaped and taught what to do. They had to participate in making movements work as they stumbled upon them in their process of discovery. The accepted discoveries had to be very concrete and had to lend themselves to the establishing of an idea. One of the recurring problems was that of space, which also became one of the most important elements in their experiments.

These were the most exciting years for Hanya, years in which her real learning and teaching started, the learning coming with the teaching, the teaching with the learning. With growing knowledge came growing abilities, and both were the result of growing experience. *Experience* became one of the key words in Hanya's vocabulary. This is why to this very day she will point out to her students and co-workers: "The most complicated and refined technique, if it does not turn into everlasting experience, will never amount to what the actual technique could be worth."

Mary Wigman depicts these years of her work with the group and with Hanya in particular:

"She belonged to the first pupils who came to me in Dresden. Of course, at that time one could not yet have spoken of a Wigman *school*. We rather were a small experimental club in which everything was tried out which the imagination would yield and which the bodily abilities would permit. But we all without exception were fanatics, obsessed with what we were doing.

"Of course, I taught my students daily. However, there were not yet any single subjects, there were not yet any systematically arranged schedules which would have organically divided the entire range of the subject matter. Whenever I was absent for a short time due to my touring obligations, the young group worked by itself and just as intensely as they would have done under my personal guidance. At my return I was surprised by a number of studies and dances on which they had worked during my absence. They were no masterpieces, of course not! After all, everything was still in the stage of its early beginning.

"On the occasion of one of our improvised dance evenings a short, delicately built girl showed her first study. "Egyptian Dance" — so it said on the program. Certainly it was derivative, there was something assimilated of seen and experienced images about it. And yet behind all this one could see an already sure feeling for style, a sense for clear organic structure and, in spite of the faults of a beginner, the ability to meet the demands on technique and body. The creative will and the ability to shape were well balanced and stood the test.

"That was Hanya and that was the first artistic impression I received from her."

Looking back at those early years now, Hanya finds it difficult to say where Mary Wigman stood then in her development. Hanya can only think of her as an artist who never remained for long at one spot, who visibly grew from work to work, from month to month. Hanya says: "She was like an ocean that always came back to you and always renewed. Her theories were not yet set. Whatever new vision came to her required a new discovery, and the question was: how shall one go about expressing this idea best? The wonderful thing in those days was that there was no preconceived method in existence, no preconceived patterns, the pattern changing with the demand and with the invention expressing the new idea. I remember, for instance, that one day the problem of vibration was brought up by the students, and I was instrumental in posing this problem. We found the answer to it while sitting on a sofa a whole night, with the springs helping us to bounce back. Then, on our feet without any outward help, the demands of the momentum carried us gradually further until the repetition of the movement finally broke down any mental opposition, and vibration became a true experience for us."

Whatever was found or discovered was the result of the cooperation of many people, and none of them would ever have thought of laying claim to this or that innovation. This joint effort was intent on making the dance a wider, a more encompassing art form. Whenever someone came up with an idea, it was never rejected out of hand but put to the test until the group found out how much value was in it. "After many weeks of studying dance composition," Hanya recalls, "everyone had a subject or was free to choose one for our so-called dance evenings. It was very helpful to present our own works, not because any one of us thought we were great choreographers, but simply to see what the chosen material did to us and what made us work on it in the first place. And the many other questions that came up: how far did it carry you, how far was it finished or remained unfinished, where was it in need of being cut or enlarged upon, and so forth. What really mattered was the concerted effort which tried to find validity in a creation and to help it become as final a work as possible. Nobody thought of himself as an originator."

Mary Wigman continues to speak of those years:
"To work with Hanya was always a pleasure and great satisfaction. She not only had a strong feeling for responsibility which gave her the strength to fulfill all tasks to perfection, she also had a marked sense for pure craftsmanship, for the detail. Her pedagogic talent was beyond any doubt, and in a relatively short time she could develop it to the point of mastery.

"Out of my first generation of students, to which Hanya belonged, I formed my first dance group — almost without my agency. Because throughout the previous period of study, during which, in the last analysis, we all were learning, we were so closely knit together that, as a result of it, the creative and artistic work became a matter of fact.

"I certainly do not want to belittle my own merits! After all, they were my artistic ideas, my form visualizations which were shaped and perfected. But the members of this first dance group were — with few exceptions — creatively gifted and contributed a great deal to the solution and to the success of each task.

"When later my solo dance tours became extended over weeks and often over months, I could leave the group in Hanya's care and be at ease because I knew that on my return I would again be able to take over the bodies of this group like instruments in faultless condition.

"As an example: the final achievement of the endurance-turns on the spot was at stake. As with everything else in a technical respect, I also had to wrest this ability from my own body — without any advice or help — I had experienced all phases of the disturbed equilibrium caused by this movement and I therefore knew what was in store for my dancers: dizziness, the loss of space awareness, and as a result of it — seasickness. Time and again the giddy bodies, the faces turning a discolored green. If I had not known that one could overcome this condition with energy and perseverance, I would not have forced all the members of my group to learn and to master this movement.

"After two weeks of my absence from Dresden I received Hanya's first report: 'We achieved an entire minute of turns!' And again two weeks later: 'Almost two minutes, and only one girl got sick.' On my return twenty young dancers stood the test for two full minutes, whirling around their own axes faultlessly. Do you know what this means? The continuum of the turning feet as if glued to the same spot, remaining at the same speed, relentlessly turning two minutes long, an eternity in whose apparent endlessness the physical existence goes through many changes and transformations of which no one ever thought: the space swinging, whipped up to a tornado . . . torrents . . . cascades . . . magnificent . . . "

In the early and middle twenties the Mary Wigman Central Institute was a genuine workshop, functioning to the benefit of master and students alike. Wigman's intelligence and ability to understand and assimilate quickly what was achieved by her co-workers became usable material for her group dances, from which, in turn, the group learned a great deal. This process created a constant flow of ideas from the student to the master, from the master to the student.

In Hanya's opinion the best creative progress can come only from group cooperation when everything is still in a condition of flux, when no movement ideas or patterns have as yet taken the form of manifested experience. At that time, she remembers, there were not yet any postulates or rules which would have predetermined the development of the creative process; there were, in her words, "no yeses and nos, no don'ts, everything was still possible; but what did not immediately work was discarded or shelved perhaps to be used at another time, in another combination, under other circumstances. There was nowhere a *verboten* sign unless it was against the principle of the movement as such, set by the body rather than by someone who made up the movement. Limitations were created by the body alone, but there was always the chance of breaking down these limitations. Also, we were always held to the art of improvisation, to a very quick, almost spontaneous, intuitive response."

But Mary Wigman saw to it that there was the necessary restraint to prevent anyone from getting lost in technique or in the emotional ocean of license. She knew how to weigh and shape form and content. She liked to build her solo dances around a very specific idea; and, with the years, her own concepts assumed an ever growing scope in depth as well as in the needed response of other dancers to herself, the bodily weight which enabled her to project certain ideas more powerfully. At the time when Hanya joined her in Dresden, Mary was working with little groups which she began to enlarge in the season of 1923–1924. She believed that the soloist's work would always remain a single and purely personal accomplishment, but that all the possibilities lay in group work. Hanya reminisces about Mary's influence in this respect:

"Mary Wigman felt that the development of every dance personality should take place in two different directions: the perfection of the performer as an individuality and, on the other hand, the adjustment of this individuality to a group.

"The dancer who choreographs may bring with him a blueprint of his idea. But this, though it may be necessary, is only the smaller part of his work. He must be so convinced of, so overwhelmed by his visualization that his own experience can become the dancer's experience and that finally a single basic chord embraces the entire group. Unlike a conductor whose co-workers play from a printed score, the choreographer works with live material, he has to utilize the creative ability without destroying the personality of the individual performer within the group.

"In the awakening of the group to a communal rhythmic pattern there lies, to some extent, self-denial of individual expression. But this yielding of ground is not lost. It is absorbed, incorporated, and brought back to life in the totality of the group's creation.

"Mary Wigman as a teacher molded independent creative life, helping other talents to mature and to become an active force in the growth of her group. She watched each individual modulation to find the one forte which every personality has. She aimed to transfer mere body into a sensitive dance instrument. This is a matter of patience, endurance, and discipline. 'Woe to the dancer who loses patience!' she once said. 'He will never find the way to the essence, to the resources and innermost motive of his dance. He will remain the self-centered Ego-Dancer whose language is masturbation. But never can he become a body of expression of all those things which, beyond his own ego, reach, embrace, and stir other people.' "

In the process of learning as well as in the creation of dance works it was the subtle and knowing hand of Mary Wigman which guided the group. In guiding these young dancers a whole set of principles evolved and, in the spirit of a community effort, theory and creative work grew to sizable and respected proportions. Hanya found a most descriptive image for the harmonious interchange when she said, "There was no dictatorship in this group which was a single body with one head, the head of the master."

A short postscriptum must be written at the end of this chapter. It is of little consequence if we believe that "that which we call a rose by any other name would smell as sweet." But names may have a mysterious meaning in the life of an artist, and an artist's name chosen at the start of his career often helps to form his profile. Often by mere chance — but do we not create the chances for chance to come our way? — a chosen name will fit what we are fit for. And in later days we may have to pose the question: How else could he or she be called? A name well chosen has the inevitability of a great work of art. Those who have known her work and known the person could not imagine Hanya Holm to be called by any other name.

In 1923 the Mary Wigman School was thronged by students from all over Europe, from Hungary, Poland, and Czechoslovakia, from Denmark, Norway, and Sweden. The bodies of these students learned to speak one and the same language, but not so their tongues. Hanya's name, Johanna Kuntze, née Eckert, lay heavily on these tongues. And Johanna was called everything else but Johanna. There were the variations Haneczka, Haniuš, Hancia, and Hanka, which finally crystallized into Hanya. "Hanya," etymologically related to the Hebrew Hannah, means grace. Now, Hanya needed an alliterative surname to give it substance, support, and greater meaning.

If "Hanya" was formed out of linguistic influences from the east and south of Germany, "Holm" derived from Nordic, purely Anglo-Saxon roots. The *holen* is our holly and appears in the holm oak; but also in dialect spoken in certain parts of England, otherwise obsolete, one can hear "holm" used for the holly. Yet more appropriate seems the Anglo-Saxon use of "holm" as hill, island, and the high sea. The most common use of the word to this day is as an islet in a river, in a lake, or near the mainland. In England it also refers to a low, flat land near a river.

At that time in Dresden Hanya only looked for a name that went well with "Hanya." The word "Holm" came up, probably mentioned by the girls from the north. Hanya liked it for the pithy sound of it. It unconsciously gave her a feeling of strength and security. She did not bother to search for its etymological roots, to find out that it was as strong as an evergreen oak tree, as wild and adventurous as the high sea, or as safe as the refuge on an islet near land. All that Hanya knew when making this choice was that this name sounded right for her.

> If one wants to achieve something, one must not have
> oneself in view, only the work, one must not want success,
> but achievement. Mistaking the person for the matter, or
> the person for the idea, leads to hidden rocks on which
> a great many artistic attempts have suffered shipwreck.
> — MARY WIGMAN
> *as quoted by Hanya Holm*

First Attempts at Creativity

MARY WIGMAN and her company performed frequently in the cities of Germany, Italy, and other countries between 1923 and 1928, but at the end of that period and despite its growing reputation, the company was beset by a seemingly irreparable financial crisis. The company had to be dissolved. The last time the members of this group were seen together was in *Celebration*, a work choreographed by Mary Wigman "for them and with them," as she declared. It was shown on the occasion of the First International Dance Congress which took place in Essen in 1928. The students of the Wigman School were also seen at this Congress in an extensive demonstration program.

It was in those critical days that Hanya was offered a leading position at the theater in Hannover. She was a young enough dancer-choreographer to be tempted by such a promising opportunity; on the other hand, her gratitude and a feeling of obligation toward Mary created a serious problem for her.

She decided to ask the advice of Mary, who in a very frank and almost impersonal manner told her: "At this point I have nothing to hold you back with. If you wish to accept it, go ahead and do it. But my advice would be to stay where you are because there is still much more for you to find out and to learn before you should expose yourself to the rough-and-tumble which is unavoidable in such a position." Hanya felt that her advice was good. She withstood the temptation and decided to stay on. It gave her the opportunity to assimilate properly what she had absorbed so far; she learned to organize her acquired knowledge, which also gave her greater security as a teacher.

Hanya remained with Mary Wigman and her sister Elisabeth as chief instructor of the school in Dresden. Mary Wigman called it "a very positive and harmonious period of creativity! The school, grown beyond its modest beginning, had achieved world reputation. Through enlargement and rebuilding of the old suburban villa the school was transformed into a dance factory and had excellent studios in which it was a pleasure to work. The students came from all over the world."

Since her schooldays Hanya had had the inclination to acquire a bit more knowledge of whatever she studied than was demanded of her. She could not help dissecting and analyzing her material until she thoroughly understood its reasons and motivations. Only then did she feel she could make up her own mind about the material in question and know what to do with it and, finally, how to present it to her students. She has never given up the digging and probing. Through trial and error, she believes, a great many things become revealed or, *nolens volens,* reveal themselves. During all the years of studying with Mary, she advanced to a position of trust from which she could function as a teacher, carrying out any task which had to be done or, when Mary was on tour, keeping the group together with the same intense readiness as shown toward the master.

This was the time when Hanya realized her own growing strength as a personality; and it was then that it became obvious to her that teaching, if meaningful, was a creative act.

But besides playing the role of chief instructor she soon had several opportunities to prove herself as a performer and choreographer. In the summers of 1928 and 1929 she was invited to choreograph and direct Euripides' *Bacchae* and a dramatization of Plato's *Farewell to His Friends* at the open-air theater in Ommen, Holland. But a more challenging and stimulating task as a performer and choreographer awaited her in 1929, when she was asked to dance the part of the Princess in Igor

Stravinsky's *L'Histoire du Soldat*. Here is Mary Wigman's eye-witness account of Hanya's first great role and how it came about:

"In the twenties, the so-called 'Golden Era of Expressionism,' Dresden was tremendously alive. On the outside it preserved the dignity and beauty of a once royal residence characterized by the age and style of the Baroque, but everything was in uproar in the artistic-cultural field: in the visual arts, in architecture and music, in the theater and dance. It virtually crackled in the decayed walls, but sparks also began to fly from one field to the other. Meetings took place which became more fruitful than could be immediately suspected. The growing and thriving Wigman School had its share in it.

"While the more traditional music-loving public in Dresden extolled Richard Strauss and the Opera premiered all his works in a festive mood, the younger generation lost its heart to the new contemporary music. The excellent pianist Paul Aron in particular made us understand modern music and taught us to *listen*, and he also worked in this spirit with our young accompanists. Hindemith and Schönberg, Satie, Krenek, and Bartok were heard, and they pushed the classics from the studios and dances of the Wigman students.

"It was Paul Aron who, in 1929, was instrumental in having Stravinsky's *L'Histoire du Soldat* staged in Dresden. Hanya was chosen to create the part of the Princess. In her first enthusiasm over having been selected for this role the counting devil got hold of her. How else could she have mastered the irregular and no longer metrical rhythms of Stravinsky's music?

"With frowning forehead bent over these notes, she studied those devilish rhythms which did not easily yield to the visual images of her dancing. But finally she succeeded in finding her way through these free-swinging rhythms, in treating them with a superior gesture and in giving to the character seen from a dancer's viewpoint the very special shape which the action of the play demanded.

"The road into a new world of music was started. It was a beautiful and successful performance — thanks to Hanya."

A year later an even greater challenge came her way when Mary Wigman became involved in the anti-war pageant, *Das Totenmal*, based on a poem and score by the Swiss poet Albert Talhoff. He had planned it as a great choric work for dance, sound, and word, but it was also supposed to be a production in which the lighting would play an equally important part. It was the concept of a mammoth work, a total-theater idea, with the dancers filling the stage, flanked by the speaking choruses on both sides. Masks, cothurni, costumes fantastic in their telling simplicity were used. There were also huge flags which phantomlike drummers had to swing. A strip of fabric, about thirteen feet long, was attached to Mary Wigman's costume and fastened on its other end to a hollow wooden stick filled with lead. This strange material could be thrown through the air, whirled tight around the body, and unfolded again like a wing. The dance action took place on several levels. Since Talhoff's ambitious lighting did not work, a compromise solution was found in creating light areas which could be dramatically separated.

Mary Wigman had cast herself in the solo part, but Hanya danced in it too and had to lead the women's chorus. "It was then," she says, "that I filled the position of a co-director. Mary entrusted me with assignments which, although I had to solve them according to her designs and wishes, gave me a great responsibility. First of all I was responsible for the whole chorus. But I had to observe everything that was going on onstage, the entire technical and artistic apparatus, which included the dancers as well as the speakers. I had to give light cues, and there were moments in this production when I had to be at the switchboard. Whenever Mary was on stage I had to pay attention to what she was doing. It was a very taxing part for Mary. This was one of the reasons why I was charged with so many different functions. At that time I was already very familiar with all the theater arts. I had acquired my stage experiences not from books but from being on stage. My beginnings with Reinhardt in Frankfort, my working in the theater in Dresden, being backstage and seeing what was going on, all this was practical experience which came in handy for the many tasks I had to fulfill in the *Totenmal*. I often had to take the initiative, my critical awareness as well as my independent judgment was challenged time and again, and decisions had to be made within seconds. For me it was decidedly a step in a new direction, and it was also my last experience on stage with Mary."

Mary Wigman says, "When I had the chance to create my first great choric work, *Das Totenmal*, in Munich, it was Hanya again who stood by me as no one else would or could have done. The one decisive characteristic of her being and doing was that she has always put the work, its idea and creation, above anything personal — giving it more meaning by serving it, even when the work as such carried unmistakably her very own artistic signature."

Hanya stayed another year as chief instructor at the Wigman School in Dresden. It was the season in which Mary Wigman made her first American tour, which led to the opening of a Wigman School in New York and to Hanya's greatest adventure: to leave her native country where she was well on the way to becoming a dancer-choreographer-teacher of great stature, and to seek the unknown in the New World.

Das Totenmal had a great impact on her. For the first time she had irrevocably come to the conclusion that the dance was to be her metier. But at that point she was not yet quite sure whether she should strive to become an important dancer, or a choreographer, or a teacher.

"When I came to Mary Wigman she asked me what I wanted to do. I said I didn't know, I'll do what I'm able to do. I never had a bigger goal in mind than the one I was sure to reach. To this very day I always tell myself I'll go as far as I can, and if the goal can be moved just a bit farther I'll go as far as that. I believe in natural growth, but in using all my faculties to the utmost while coasting along. I suppose this started in my schooldays when I learned to paint, to play the piano, when my voice and body were somewhat trained. Very early my appetite for the arts had been whetted and my desire grew to get better acquainted with them. It was natural for me in those years to go to the theater, to concerts, to the opera and museums as often as I could. There was no purpose, no preconceived thought in doing these things. I did not intend to sharpen my critical judgment or to feed my sensibilities. I only did these things because I enjoyed them. That I gained by doing so was my good fortune."

A NEW WORLD

I have denied myself a great deal to achieve discipline.

— HANYA HOLM

Six Years of Preparation

AFTER Mary Wigman's first transcontinental tour in America, her impresario, Sol Hurok, came to visit her in Dresden. This was his first acquaintance with the Wigman School. He was deeply impressed by what he saw, and his enterprising mind immediately recognized the great promise of a Wigman School in New York. He thought that the young barefoot dancers in America who had just begun to try their wings would flock to her school now that they had seen Wigman dance. Hurok became so enthusiastic that he decided on the spot to have a branch of the Wigman School in the New World.

Mary Wigman warned him that a school is not part of show business; that it cannot be engaged like an artist; that an educational institute, responsible in its work, must be given a chance to grow through many years. But Hurok's enthusiasm could not be curbed. He visualized the great contribution this school would make to the development of the American modern dance, he felt instinctively that it would be a great success. And when he sensed success, no one could stop Sol Hurok. History proved him right long after he had lost interest in the school.

"Hanya was also quite excited about this idea," Mary Wigman recalled, "and I knew that among all my students she would be the only one who could be trusted with supervising a New York school. And this is how Hanya came to America."

It was on September 25, 1931, in the afternoon, that Hanya landed on the shores of America. The *Aquitania* had deposited her at the pier at West 14th Street. Immediately after her arrival she gave an interview in which she said: "It takes time to become a dancer, the art must grow within you while your body is learning to move." It was as if she had set these words as the motto for the next years to come.

Among the many immigrants who, year after year, have added new substance to the proverbial melting pot, Hanya Holm was destined to create an important place for herself in the New World. By the same token, she was to contribute to the modern dance in America the fourth wheel which enabled it to move forward full blast and establish itself in the artistic and educational field all over the country.

She went through the emotional seesaw stages familiar to most immigrants. In the very beginning she was in a state of euphoria. Her first year in New York was the easiest. Carried on the wings of Sol Hurok's impresarioship and profiting from Mary Wigman's successes while here on tour, Hanya had her honeymoon with America. On first nodding acquaintance she found the American people warm and hospitable, and the dancers as cordial as she, the stranger, could expect. She had no immediate struggles or worries since Sol Hurok held his protective hand over her and the Mary Wigman School; he steered the ship, from his administrative post, with his usual efficiency. Besides, it was easy sailing. The school was a novelty and, as happens with most novelties, it turned out to be the drawing card which Mr. Hurok had envisioned. Most dancers wanted to see for themselves what the "famous" Wigman technique was like, how it felt to move the "German" way.

It was quite different the second year. Sol Hurok, the born impresario, soon found out that playing the administrative headmaster, with the many cumbersome little chores entailed in such a position, was different from the initially inspiring launching of a school. He tired of being tied down by a responsibility removed from his ambitions. Hanya did not think it right to cajole him into staying with the school. She then realized that she was on her own and she "had" to make a go of it. After all, he had introduced her to the American dancers, she felt, and that was all she could expect from him. His decision was certainly understandable from his point of view, and it has always been Hanya's fortune — or sometimes misfortune — to see both sides of a coin. But she also recognized immediately that what she was left with was hard on her.

The school had no deficit the first year and it had to be bought from Mr. Hurok. Hanya did not have the necessary means, but friends of Mary Wigman and some of those whom Hanya had meanwhile befriended were ready to help. But to run a school and to build up a following is a long-range program which needs substantial financial backing. Moreover, in the second year the school was no longer *le dernier cri*. It was a bitter realization for Hanya to acquaint herself with an attitude of which she, as the thorough and painstaking worker, could not approve. "After one year they thought they knew it all," she reminisces. "What went particularly against my grain was the fact that so many of those who had come to study with me the first year were people in teaching positions, or who had already made some kind of a name for themselves — and they thought that this passing acquaintanceship with the Wigman method was enough. Well, it wasn't in my eyes, and I was afraid that some of them might even dare teach what they thought they knew."

With considerably fewer students at hand, Hanya was well aware of having to start from the very beginning. And she began — or continued — with a different aim in mind, visualizing the difficulties she would have to overcome. Somebody else might have lost courage and returned to her native land where she was sure of her position with Mary and where she knew she could have made her way easily. Also, almost simultaneously with Sol Hurok's offer, she had had the possibility of teaching in Russia, a chance she had forgone in favor of being able to work in America. This opening might still have been waiting for her.

Hanya went back to Germany in the summer of 1932. It was not with the intent of staying there, but to exchange her American visitor's visa for an immigration visa, a formality necessary for obtaining citizenship. She had decided by then to become an American. She was determined to fight it out here. "I started with the awareness," she says, "that in order to prove what I could do I had to show it. I wanted to develop a small group, not with any big artistic aims, a demonstration company only. And the first thing I did was to work on a dance demonstration program."

It is characteristic of her that in settling down in America she did not immediately rush into creative work — and this in spite of her success in *L'Histoire du Soldat* and *Das Totenmal*, which had given her hope for a possibly great career. No, she sat back and tried to absorb what was going on around her, gradually adjusting herself to her new environment.

The first two years of teaching turned into her own *Lehrjahre*. She was fully aware that in order to be able to teach she had to learn about the people, she had to know what made them react the way they did. She gathered a few of the people who had been with her from the very beginning, drew them closer to work with them toward the planned demonstration program. It took her almost five years to get a dependable company together, but a unit of dancers as a working group was more easily achieved. These dancers, she felt, would become the exponents of the basic ideas of what dance was to her.

"Therefore I could not only say, Do this or that, it had to be understood as the principle of what I wanted to have done. This meant a very thorough training, not just the customary physical training, an indoctrination, I would say. To me, dancing is a way of thinking. At the same time this was for me a period of learning, of absorbing how I could get my ideas across, on how fertile a soil my seed would fall, where the resistance lay, which concepts were conveniently changed to fit my students' thinking and understanding. They, of course, did not realize how much I was learning while teaching them. There were people from the old country, most of them second generation, and people from Asia, and the spirit, the atmosphere in which they existed and which they carried with them was very different from what I knew.

"At first, I was taken aback by their points of view, by their philosophy of life. The feeling that nothing is impossible, that everything goes, the opportunistic attitude and the one that you can buy what you want, and, after all, their idea so often expressed in their gestures: I pay for my class, so you go and show me — all this I had to learn and fight. I tried to make them understand that there was more to it than buying, that you had to give your entire being, that you had to look into the depth of an idea and had to look deep into it until you were sure you no longer got dizzy from doing so."

Hanya also realized that New York was not America, and she began to travel immediately. She went west. In the summer of 1933 she taught at the Perry Mansfield Camp near Steamboat Springs. She was deeply impressed by the austere majesty of the Colorado mountains, by the freedom of the endless plains. Then she went farther, to the West Coast, and California was again a different experience to her. She plunged herself into the realities of this new world, she could not see and listen enough to all the many new impressions and voices which puzzled and enchanted her.

"I was very eager to learn what makes America tick," she says, "from the cowboy to the legendary gold-digger to the sophisticated San Franciscan. I went to New Orleans and Boston. I was in Iowa and marveled at the huge fields on which the pigs are running around, and I was surprised about the completely different mentality of the people there — with the stress on nature, on agriculture — from the people's mentality in San Francisco, which has a touch of the Orient and which, at the same time, is probably the most European city in the States. These discrepancies taught me a great deal since they don't exist in Germany. There the peasant is different from the city-dweller as everywhere else, but his outlook on life, his cultural background is in no way marked as it is here. But even a San Franciscan I found to be very different from a New Yorker."

She had the opportunity to teach at Mills College on the West Coast and in Denver, Aspen, and Colorado Springs during the summer months. Hanya loved nature and loved to escape the narrow confines of New York City. Being so far west, she even ventured on a trip to Hawaii. There was an insatiable desire in her to absorb everything that is American. Within the first five or six years she acquired enough knowledge of country and people to give her an understanding of the entire continent. "I had a very good idea of what America was like," she stresses, "but I realized I knew very little in detail although I kept my eyes and ears open all the time. I knew that the process of absorption — through whatever osmosis it is made possible — takes a long time."

During the seasons in New York she was just as eager to learn as she was during her travels. This cosmopolitan city offered many spiritual adventures to her. She walked through the city as if wonders were hiding behind each street corner, as if a new world were waiting to be discovered by her day and night. In the evenings she used to walk along Broadway in order to get a feeling for the pulsebeat of the city. She would sit through newsreels, often twice, only to listen to the language, its intonation and pronunciation. To improve her English she caught herself quite unconsciously repeating aloud idiomatic phrases and sentences which she had just heard. In these first years there was constantly something happening to her, something she would pick up here or take in there. But all this was done without any nervous haste. In a very simple and quiet way she absorbed bit by bit what this strange new environment had to offer her. Every detailed experience helped shape her outlook on her new life, sharpened her viewpoints toward a better knowledge of how to proceed in bringing what she had to say most convincingly to the understanding of her students and the members of her demonstration group.

She was fully aware of the fact — it was fascinating to her to watch herself — that month after month she added new shades to shed old habits from her former being "made in Germany." She learned how to moderate and modulate one aspect or to intensify another; she realized that she began to elaborate on certain things in a different way than she would have dealt with the same problem in Europe. There was more to it than merely changing from one language to another. Language also helps form one's thoughts, English being far more precise and direct than German and demanding a less circumstantial thinking than the German mind is accustomed to. But this mysterious verbal transformation is a slow and in certain ways a lifelong process; to this very day she often falls into the habit of speaking a characteristic Hanya Holm English, a peculiar amalgam of the old and new Hanya. But besides and beyond the linguistic problem, it was the entire cultural climate which she loved and which accelerated her Americanization. The vision of the New York skyline with the horizon of endless distances behind it was a vision with which she lived and which gave her the strength to say Yes to her adopted country.

But however decisive the changes in her were, they were in no way radical. The leaves and some branches of the tree of her life changed, the branches acquiring more resilience, the leaves livelier coloring; also the tree learned to bend with the winds, far more powerful and vigorous than those she was accustomed to in Europe. But the trunk remained the same, it relied on its old roots absorbing the sap with its habitual intensity from the new soil.

In the first few years of Hanya's stay in America it happened more often than not that she was questioned about the intrinsic differences between the German and the American modern dance. Due to Mary Wigman's success during both her transcontinental tours, in 1930–1931 and 1931–1932, dancers discussed these differences heatedly. The German modern dance, about a decade older than its American counterpart, had the advantage of experience and greater technical solidification. At the end of the 1920s, when Mary Wigman and other German dancers had already accumulated a rich repertoire and had some memorable accomplishment behind them, the American pioneers were still fighting in an awesome artistic wilderness to find an indigenous form and expression of their own dream. Martha Graham gave her first recital in 1926; Doris Humphrey made her debut in New York in 1928, joining forces with Charles Weidman. In the previous year Helen Tamiris had given her first concert. But by then Mary Wigman's repertoire already consisted of forty-five solos and sixteen group works.

But rarely did these discussions reveal any real depth of perception, moving on a rather superficial level of comparisons and criticism, simply because the debaters lacked the understanding of the deeper motivations of Wigman's technique and the knowledge of her background. However, the very fact of the frequent juxtapositions of the American and German interpretations of the art was indicative of the interest aroused and never quite satisfied. The similiarities of these two art expressions were more readily recognized than their contrasts. Nobody denied their spiritual kinship and their existence as artistic reaction to identical or analogous forces active at that time. But only a few understood the constitutionally different sources leading to different results.

To explain the meaning of the German dance in the American scene and its possible impact on it was one of Hanya's formidable tasks in and out of her school. She was then often invited to speak on this subject which, of course, would come up time and again on her college tours. But there were lectures to be delivered at The New School — these lectures were at that time under the auspices of John Martin — at Columbia University, and at many other institutes of learning. Hanya always stressed the point that the good and honest teacher transplanted to a new country cannot afford to observe, he must rather participate and he must not maintain past achievements and standards at the expense of further progress through absorption and assimilation. As far as she was concerned, pliability was an essential gift of the teacher.

But such attitudes neither helped to explain away nor to remove the great differences between the two techniques and interpretations, and Hanya always felt that they should be aired as openly and as often as possible. With regard to the European and American artists, there were of course fundamental differences in the very approach to art itself. There were, above all, the haste and vital drive of the American artist in contrast to the marked sense of tolerance and patience for slow and gradual growth of the European artist, who would more easily dare develop through error and trial, with less fear of failures on his way to himself. Also, in such lectures Hanya pointed out that the age and youth of the respective cultures here and there imply vast differences and that America grew much faster in the mechanical and industrial fields than the European countries, which, on the other hand, were burdened with dissent and wars — and both having their specific influence on art and artist.

She summed up her ideas in an essay* in which she dramatically juxtaposed the existing and then hotly debated differences between the principles of Mary Wigman and those of the American modern dancers:

The entire orientation of Mary Wigman's dance is toward the establishment of a relationship between man and his universe. It is this philosophical tendency that influences the emotional, spatial and functional aspects of her own dancing and her pedagogical principles. Emotionally the German dance is basically subjective and the American dance objective in their characteristic manifestations. This is of course a generalization and as such true only to the point of exceptions, but I believe it throws some light on their fundamental emotional departure. The tend-

* *Modern Dance*, edited by Virginia Stewart. New York: E. Weyhe, 1935.

ency of the American dancer is to observe, portray and comment on her surroundings with an insight into intellectual comprehension and analysis. This applies to the foremost and most recent examples in this country. Up to the present the trend was toward either the purely pictorial and decorative or the predominantly functional.

The German dancer, on the other hand, starts with the actual emotional experience itself and its effect upon the individual. The distinction is one of "being" as contrasted with "doing" — of immersing the self in an emotional state as the necessary prelude to creation as contrasted with objective reconstruction of a known situation. Each of these approaches have their potential weaknesses and individual strengths. In the American method there is a danger of straying so far from the source in its reality that the final product loses in warmth and communicable fervor whatever it may have gained in perception. The dangers of looseness of form, obscurity are inherent in the German dance, and the attendant evils of mere self-expression. Properly controlled, however, within its medium, this approach lends depth, radiance, and emotional conviction to the dancer's efforts. Properly disciplined, I believe that the awakening and stimulation of confidence in instinct and emotion can be a valuable contribution to the education of the American dancer. The German pedagogical technique employs for this end improvisation on emotional as well as functional themes aimed first at freedom of expression but ultimately toward integrated composition. Without form we cannot speak of art, but the form must be an integral, not a superimposed, part of the whole and must flow unmistakably with that inner flame which is its source and its significance.

This subjective and emotional approach colors even more subtly the use of space characteristic of the German dancer, it accounts at least in part for the greater consciousness of space, actual and created as a factor of tremendous importance. Space, rhythm, volume, proportion are realized both by the American and the German dancer of first rank. But the use of space as an emotional element, as active partner in the dance, is distinctly European. For us, possibly because of a past more complex and a destiny more at the mercy of outer forces than is the case in America, we have become aware of the dramatic implications in the vision of the individual pitted against the universe. Space with its constrictions and its immensity, its dark vistas and blinding horizons becomes for the dancer an invitation or a menace, but in any case an inescapable element. The American dancer seems frequently to have little use, to be but slightly aware of space except as an incidental factor in design and floor pattern. Perhaps it is because the American background has had no external obstructions to their conquest of the vastness of their continent, because distances have succumbed with relatively little struggle to the pioneer's onward march that the American dancer stands above and so often untouched by space as an active agent.

Mary Wigman, from whose genius and early experiments the entire German dance derived its present standing, illustrates perfectly its intimate feeling for space. Those of us who worked with her at the start of her career will be forever permeated with those fundamental principles toward which she has always striven. In the realm of space particularly, I feel that Mary Wigman has made a great contribution to the contemporary dance. In her dances she alternately grapples with space as an opponent and caresses it as though it were a living, sentient thing. In her gestures and movements she carves boldly and delicately visible and fluid forms, shaping, surrounding, and sinking in the space which presses close about her.

Similarly, this emotional impetus makes felt its influence even in the physical techniques of the moving body. Superb and precise as is the technical virtuosity of even the less than great American dancers, their approach and interest are usually directed toward bodily accomplishment for its own sake. Even though a given dance may be composed to convey an emotional theme the mechanics used in its externalization are separately developed. A gesture and movement vocabulary are first prepared and only subsequently employed in various combinations for various ends. This can be done with finished and brilliant results, but it is an approach radically different from that of the German dancer. For us each composition evolves through its own emotional demands not only its spatial gestures but more important still its particular tension and even its distinctive technique. Naturally the preliminary training of the dancer is based upon a physical as well as an emotional development but its scope is general rather than specific in aim. The functions of the moving body, moreover, are felt rather than visualized and the whole being encouraged to participate rather than merely to direct. Particularly indicative of this tendency is the use of what we have called "states" of movement as an instrument for emotional freedom and enlarged and revitalized horizons in movement concepts.

These principles which are incorporated in the educational

method of Mary Wigman have, I believe, much that will be worthwhile to the American dancer. Through her the existence and importance of the eternal source of dancing — sensed by many others at this time — is made articulate. Realizing the error and futility of teaching dance forms in themselves, her credo leaves open all question of personal or national systems and results, and is content to point out the underground springs that wait to be tapped by the individual artist. In America, more perhaps than anywhere else in the world today, there waits fresh and vigorous material for the dance. In its environment and in the temperament and vitality of its people the future American dance has an enviable heritage.

It was in those early years that Hanya had to make a weighty decision. After 1933 and Hitler's seizure of power in Germany, the mood in America and particularly among the modern dancers in New York was strongly anti-Nazi and waxed with every news of Hitler's dictatorial madness and the ensuing growingly disturbing acts of violence. Also, many suspected Mary Wigman of having given in to Nazism since she had neither left Germany nor publicly detached herself from the regime. Her school was still functioning, and she went on to create new works for herself and her group, which continued to give recitals.

The pressures in New York became so strong that in November 1936 Hanya wrote Mary Wigman that the anti-Nazi mood made it impossible to keep the school alive under the name of "Mary Wigman." It is again characteristic of Hanya's integrity and loyalty that, at that point, she still left the decision to Mary whether she should give up the school and return to Germany or stay on nevertheless. "For me there was no doubt as to what she should do," Mary Wigman reminisced. "I replied to her letter: if you gained a foothold over there and if you would like to stay — by all means erase the name Mary Wigman and call it the Hanya Holm School. Hanya certainly never regretted having made this step, and I was happy about it."

This is how the Hanya Holm School of Dance came into being. Hanya felt that, with the change of the school's name, a
public declaration was desirable, which she worded as follows:

> American artistic circles have approached me with the request
> to make an open declaration of my political convictions.
>
> This school which Mary Wigman founded and I have built
> up has as its foundation her philosophy, but has always been an
> independent institution. Mary Wigman's visits in the years 1931
> and 1932, in the capacity of a consultant, were artistically and
> pedagogically of great value, but time and distance have auto-
> matically brought about a complete dissociation. When I under-
> took the directorship of the school it was a self-understood
> premise that tolerance and creative freedom must be the pre-
> requisites of the artist.
>
> With full conviction I still adhere to this concept. A racial
> question or a political question has never existed and shall never
> exist in my school. In my opinion there is no room for politics in
> art. I most emphatically refuse to identify myself with any
> political creed which strangles the free development of art, re-
> gardless of whether these political straitjackets are imported from
> Europe or manufactured here.
>
> I take this occasion to make public the announcement that the
> school which I am directing shall from now on go under my own
> name. This decision has become necessary in order to prevent
> misunderstanding, although my respect and admiration for the
> artist Mary Wigman is today the same as ever.

Essentially, what Hanya Holm discovered and rediscovered
in these first few years was that most of the Wigman principles
were incontestable, but that the Wigman themes had little to do
with the American temperament. She realized that the application of all that was found in the wellsprings of dance potential
had to be changed for the American mentality. More and more
she insisted on developing the pure instrument of the body to
enable it to go from there wherever it wanted to.

This became one of the pivotal points of her technique
classes, and many of the dancers who came from Hanya went
their own ways successfully without denying the heritage they

had taken with them. Another novelty she introduced was the use of improvisation. In the way Hanya practiced it, it had been unknown in America and had all the earmarks of the German technique. She extended greatly the range of these improvisation classes. One of her students, Alwin Nikolais, said about them: "We had long sessions of improvisation, not the cathartic type. They were to me like a corridor of thought through which the mind propels itself, causing action to take place in a scheme very much like jazz improvisation."

Also Hanya's attitude toward choreography changed in these years, basically because of the drama that went on in the mysterious "within-ness" of a growing human being. It of course included the drama between person and person, between the German and the American mentality, this invisible struggle between continent and continent which rapidly ripened her experiences. As one of the results of this struggle she moved noticeably away from the Wigman style, essentially dramatic, toward a freer and more lyrical style through which she was able to come more easily closer to what could loosely be described as the American spirit.

Hanya has had many "firsts" in her career as an artist, but so had she as a teacher. She was one of the first to stress the interrelation of the subject areas with the knowledge of the body. The logical next step was to have anatomy taught in her studio. She had never forgotten the experiences she had gathered in her days with Dalcroze, and in order to heighten her students' kinesthetic sensations to rhythm she offered a special percussion training. Hanya also told her students that it was essential for them to widen their mental horizon as best they could to have the most encompassing knowledge about the close affinity between the various art forms, and she would often interrupt her classes, particularly her theory classes, with ideas associated with the other arts. It was from her viewpoint self-evident that one has to relive history if one is not fully aware of it, as George Santayana pointed out. To give her students deeper insight into the past and its social function she would prove her wide frame of reference by citing examples of previous days; and at one time she had John Martin, then dance critic of *The New York Times*, teach dance history in her studio.

She established herself first as a teacher, and she did so quite consciously, knowing only too well that she came to the States as the head of a school and with the message which this school was expected to deliver to the New World. It was as a teacher with a philosophy — though Germanic in background and shaped by Wigman concepts — which, with the years, became so markedly *the* Hanya Holm philosophy of the dance. It was in many ways different from, or almost alien to, what had been developing on American soil. Her insight into human nature and her ability to give it full realization as a teacher were her forte. Moreover, while giving her students a far-reaching freedom, she helped them overcome their limitations. She brought with her a new concept of spatial architecture.

She was the first one to travel the college circuit extensively and the first one to do it with a demonstration program that had artistic *Gestalt*. It was Hanya who, during the thirties, popularized the modern dance in the "hinterland," conquering virgin soil for this then new art form, creating an appreciation for the "barefoot" dancers — the same as Anna Pavlova once did for the ballet consciousness of the American people when, beginning in World War I and through the twenties, she often toured the States and was seen in the smallest places. "Going to these small places," Hanya says, "I was surprised to find that these first-rate colleges were equipped for all kinds of physical activities but that dance was only accepted when it was ballet, ballroom, tap, or jazz. It was real pioneering in those days, and we literally took our lives into our hands. The youngsters in the audience were not easily satisfied, they answered back with firecrackers or popped balloons. But I kept my talking to a minimum and tried to catch their attention with action. We made many of these college tours. I suppose we did get through to them after all since to this very day I have met people, nondancing people, who tell me that they saw me on stage out in the Midwest in the thirties when they went to college. Our demonstration programs must have made some impression on them that they had not forgotten."

In the main, Hanya played around in these programs with improvisations which turned into little compositions in etude form. Her theater sense made it possible to have even such exercises in creativity built up sequentially and dramatically. She would begin with very plain and simple movement sequences, constantly growing more complicated and developing toward a final point. But the road taken and the goal reached did not aim at any pretentious level of artistic achievement; everything undertaken was on a modest scale. She had a few exercises on the floor first and, in building them up, they led into vertical stress, pliés, and swinging. There was an etude on a straight and one on a curved path, an etude dealing with elevation, with soundless dance as well as with dance to percussion, an etude on falls, on gravity and the resistance to it, on centrifugal and centripetal force, and other studies which created — as her teaching still does — a base of natural spatial laws which permits each individual to relate to it personally. All these exercises grew into compositional form and assumed the feeling of an exploratory journey into a land of revelations.

These demonstration programs were illustrative, almost dreamlike in their lyric molding of space and mood, but, above all, they gave the audiences what all audiences love — a keyhole view of an art. These demonstrations became such favorites with audiences everywhere that Hanya could not comfortably omit them even when her programs consisted only of compositional numbers. Usually the second section of the program would include her demonstration etudes.

Walter Terry, who was then dance critic at the *Boston Herald*, can still remember having been impressed by these demonstrations:

"I saw some demonstrations in Boston. She was very good at that, and one of these etudes, *Dance of Introduction*, was created as a final demonstration for such a dance demonstration

HANYA HOLM AND HER DANCE GROUP
DEMONSTRATION PROGRAM
Accompanist—HARVEY POLLINS

PART I

TYPES OF FUNDAMENTAL DANCE MOVEMENT

RELAXATION (in swing form)
Progression from head through body to feet, lower leg and whole leg, using forward, backward and sideward combinations.
Development in volume of movement and in tension, beginning with the hip swing.
Rhythmic elements in group and solo forms.

ELASTICITY
Starting with the plain skip followed by various forms of the skip into the leap.
Solo improvisations on the skip and the leap.
Development of the leap through a crescendo use of energy.

PART II

THE SIGNIFICANCE
of direction and space in the dance, presented in etude form.
(*These are in no way finished dances but merely studies to illustrate the various problems.*)

1 Etude on straights and curves.
Circle dissolving into single floor patterns.
Angular paths.
Curved paths.

2 Volume and space dimensions resulting from:
(*a*) Pulsating group movement (without music)
(*b*) Active dynamic movement

3 Etude on passivity
Movement through levels of space

4 Solo studies in space
Harmonious relation between dancer and space
Carolyn Durand

Space shattered by explosive quality arising from inner excitement of the dancer whose body is the focal point
Lucretia Barzun

Conflict between the attractions of two opposing focal points   *Elizabeth Waters*

Space as scenery suggested through descriptive movement
Dora Brown

Effervescent movement motivated by excitement coloring space   *Henrietta Greenhood*

Attraction toward depth   *Bernice van Gelder*

Suspension   *Louise Kloepper*

5 Resurgent plunging into depth   *Group*

6 "Primitive Rhythm" (*from the Concert Program*)
Miss Holm and Group

A Typical "Demonstration Program" as Presented in Hartford.

program. She was always very clear about this business of dynamics, of centering the body, of use of breath and being in space. Jerome Robbins once said that too often dance creators think of space as emptiness and it is not, it is volume. Whether he learned that from Hanya or whether he arrived at that by himself, I don't know. Hanya uses space as volume, and whenever I do my own lecture-demonstrations I show how a ballet dancer moves through space — he walks through — but a modern dancer makes use of the drama of space, of its volume. And in my dance demonstrations I use actually some of Hanya's exercises because they do display the progress of the body, not just the wandering of the body, but the body determined to go in a certain direction. With Hanya it was the architecture, the form, the intensity which I remember specifically."

At such group lecture-demonstrations Hanya's words were kept to a minimum, simply referring to space consciousness as a phase of importance in the modern dance. "Dance movement is projected through space, in space and with space. It does not stop with the audience. It goes beyond. It goes as far as the dancer's intensity sends it." Hanya would also allude to the fact that the audience perceives kinesthetically and emotionally more than it sees: "The dimensions of a movement expand in planes, travel through levels of space, and it is this extension that touches you in passing. The contact is of universal, not personal, significance. The reaction is bigger than the dance, the dancer, or the audience. It is an unvoiced conversation among many people concerning the inexpressible affairs of man." These demonstrations showed the development from first precepts of relaxation to the problems of conquering space. They were exercises yet not mere exercises. This is why Hanya came to call them etudes, and among the space studies, both for solo and groups, the movements she employed ran the gamut from passive identification with surrounding space to an explosive shattering of it.

Only in the very beginning, when Hanya was not yet quite sure of her English and when circumstances forced her into a defensive mood, did she read her introductory speeches from a manuscript. One of them found among old papers ran as follows:

Because of so much confusion concerning modern art generally and modern dance particularly, it may add to the enjoyment of tonight's program if we try to make clear just what modern dance means to us as students of dance.

Of course the dance or art of any age is modern in its time; therefore the term "modern" is rather unfortunate; but when we stop to compare the dances of today with the forms of earlier times, we must admit that there are outstanding differences which make it necessary to use some differentiating term. The trends that have caused the recent developments in dance are the same as those observed in all cultural forms. With dance, as with all the arts, the greatest change has been due perhaps to the radical changes in the philosophy of aesthetics since the eighteenth century and to a deepening knowledge of the medium of dance, which is movement. Today we are developing and perfecting techniques according to forms that are inherent in movement itself rather than techniques developed for visual appearance alone. Such an approach to technique makes for a movement quality that is more vital and organic than the artificial prettiness that typed the dancing of the recent past. Our danger is in going to the other extreme, resulting in meaningless grotesquerie. Although we are not imitating and copying these earlier forms, it does not mean that they have nothing of interest and value for us, for they are indeed an integral part of our rich art heritage from the past. It means rather that in the light of modern science and philosophy, they are no longer the answers to the artistic needs of present-day life.

So the modern movement in dance cannot be detached from the general course of culture. Modern thought and sentiment are reflected in all the patterns of life, whether it be art, politics, religion, or social reform. But it must be remembered that the true artist is never partisan. Art is the expression and communication of an artistic treatment reflecting the personality of the artist. One is an artist regardless of nationality, creed, or political affiliation, and despite the fact that his creation is affected by his general philosophy of life.

In this evening's recital the attempt has been made to express and communicate in movement our reactions to life's experiences as artistically as possible with what understanding and ability we have at our command. Perhaps it would be simpler if you would think of us as modern students dancing rather than students presenting the modern dance.

These years in the thirties were years of preparatory nature. They were full of hard, exploratory work. They defended a viewpoint while developing a constantly growing personal *Lebensphilosophie*. They finally led to an impressive work, *Trend*, with which Hanya established herself as a choreographer of stature. "It was the first of the bigger compositions," Hanya says, "one with a solid concept which had a contemporaneous, perhaps I should rather say a timeless, content."

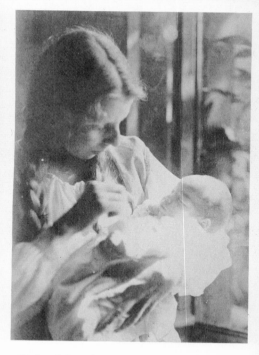

1. (a) A Window in Dresden: Hanya Holm, Mary Wigman, Elisabeth Wigman. (b) *Totenmal*: Hanya Holm in Costume, with Mask. (c) Mother and Son, the 1920s: Hanya Holm and Klaus.

2. *Totenmal*: Men's and Women's Choruses.

3. (a) *Totenmal*: Hanya Holm and Cast during a Break in Re-
hearsal, Munich. (b) New York: Louise Kloepper, Nancy McKnight
Hauser, and Hanya Holm. (c) Bennington: Louis Horst, Louise
Kloepper, Hanya Holm, Martha Graham.

4. (a) Colorado Springs: Alwin Nikolais, Hanya Holm. (b) Perry-Mansfield Camp, Colorado: Hanya Holm, Valerie Bettis.

I have never run away from any issue. Wherever I arrived, I have always reached my destination through struggling with myself. Everything came out of experience. I have never been able to do anything out of a book.

— HANYA HOLM

"Trend" and the Modern Dance in America

In the early thirties the American dance was coming into its own. In the field of the ballet, companies were founded, such as the Littlefield Ballet in Philadelphia in 1935, the first ballet group made up of and directed entirely by Americans. In 1933 Lincoln Kirstein had invited George Balanchine to come to the States to establish with him the School of American Ballet. Its outgrowth, the American Ballet, made its first appearance in Hartford, Connecticut, in 1934 and a few months later at the Adelphi Theatre in New York with seven ballets by George Balanchine. In the spring of 1936 Lincoln Kirstein also founded the Ballet Caravan, a group which had the distinction of stressing American themes as in Lew Christensen's *Filling Station* and *Pocahontas* and Eugene Loring's *Billy the Kid*. Michel Fokine had his school in New York and so had Mikhail Mordkin, from whose company emerged Lucia Chase's American Ballet Theatre. Ruth Page and Bentley Stone came from Chicago and prepared their minds and bodies for such American folkloric material as *Americans in Paris, Hicks at the Country Fair, An American Pattern*, later followed by *Frankie and Johnny* and *Billy Sunday*. Long before Agnes de Mille created *Rodeo* she was seen in a solo, *Civil War*, as early as 1929.

Ballet certainly had been flexing its muscles. It was a period of general awakening toward a yet undreamt-of greatness.

This was paralleled by the new movement of the modern dance, which, in its barefoot, unadorned simplicity and self-expressive manner, went its own way. The modern dance was throbbing with excitement at that time, the excitement of great experimentation which was not yet quite sure of where it was going, although it was certain that its destiny was to give America an indigenous theater dance. The modern dance was to complete the dream that Isadora Duncan's artistic promise had left unfulfilled.

The stress in both ballet and the modern dance was on America, on her spirit and folkloric atmosphere, on the vigor and athletic strength of her dancers. The American spirit found its expression in most of the themes and in the approach to subject matter. There was an unvoiced pride in leading America toward the forefront of the dance world.

After beginning with choreographic attempts reflecting varied interest and a groping for the bigger theme and a more satisfactory subject matter, Martha Graham turned in the early 1930s to American Indian material and American behavior patterns. She prepared the way for her folkloristic classic, *Appalachian Spring*, with a series of American themes: *American Provincials, Frontier, Primitive Mysteries, Two Primitive Canticles, American Document*, and *Ceremonials*. Supported by her mentor, Louis Horst, she began to define her technique of contraction and release. Of all the modern dancers at that time it was Martha Graham who dominated the scene and exerted the greatest influence, if for no other reason than that she was the most glamorous figure and the strongest performer.

With the exception of *The Shakers*, created in 1931, *American Holiday*, 1938, and *Square Dances*, 1939, Doris Humphrey was far more interested in universal themes than in folkloric ones. But in her attempt at exploring human relationships as well as in her approach to human and socially significant statements she was very American. She, too, established new technical principles, her theory of fall and recovery, applying her idea of movement as an "arc between two deaths" in her work as a creative artist and teacher. Her partner, Charles Weidman, with whom she founded a school and concert company in 1927, was far more American-oriented than Doris. Before he arrived at his Lincoln work, *A House Divided* —, he had choreographed *American Saga* in 1935, and *Lynch Town* as well as *Traditions* in 1936.

Helen Tamiris, a maverick in the modern dance field and, strangely enough, never embraced by the three great modern dancers, helped establish an America-directed atmosphere with *American Moods* and her famous Negro *Spirituals* as early as 1929, and later in the thirties, during the period of the Federal Theatre Project, she choreographed *How Long, Brethren*, set to Negro songs of protest; *Liberty Song*, a theme of the American Revolution; and the suite of *Bayou Ballads*.

It is well to keep this situation in mind when we try to visualize Hanya's entrance on this scene. As little as one is considered a prophet in one's own country, one is, on the other hand, very easily held an intruder on foreign soil. One can be given credit for what one stands for. But, in the last analysis, if one does not speak the same idiomatic tongue, one will be unable to participate in the shared laughter and unembarrassed silences of people with a different background in common. Also, it is not easy to find one's way in an alien environment, and one's own uncertainties and bewilderment may cause conjecture and impose an unwanted feeling of wariness.

The strongly America-oriented stress was only too natural for the modern dance movement and its leading individualists. It undoubtedly helps to give the artist a greater security to go back to his roots when on the path of any daring new exploration. This is all the more understandable in the case of the American modern dancers, who rightly felt that they had found their own idiomatic dance language, independent from what had preceded them by a decade in Europe.

The second and third years of Hanya's activities in America were probably the hardest for her and would have been for anyone in her position, even with more understanding of the situation and with more willingness to become a part of the whole. What John Martin wrote in his *Introduction to the Dance*, published in 1939, undoubtedly shortened Hanya's period of probation in this country and determined at least some of the reactions in her favor:

> She spread her roots in her new environment and eagerly invited its influences. Such an approach was totally different from what America was accustomed to from European artists, for they have all too frequently brought with them an overbearing arrogance and a determination to teach a nation of barbarians how to become civilized. Holm's gentleness and humility marked her as clearly not of this kind; her interest was not to impose her ideas upon America, but quite to the contrary, to allow its vitality and freshness to bring her art to maturity.

It helped Hanya a great deal to suppress the urge of the creative artist during her self-imposed period of waiting, to avoid the clash of egos where it hurts most: in the public arena where artistry must be proved. On the level of teaching the competition was still strong enough to cause misunderstandings which, in turn, caused frictions. "In the beginning my isolation, or a recognizable feeling of animosity, which my coming and being here created, was more than understandable — though to understand it did not keep me from feeling the hurt," Hanya says. "As the saying has it, all new brooms sweep better, this is why so many people came to find out the *difference* and everyone was interested in what was really behind this new method coming from abroad. It is quite logical — particularly seeing things in retrospect — that curiosity should turn into critical appraisal. I had to accept it at that time and do understand now why my method was rejected in many circles."

Artistic feuds of this kind, which not only expose ideas but also involve human beings, a following, and students, are never fought out on an esoteric plane. It is not only a matter of the assertion of one's ideas and ego, it often means bread and butter at the same time. In the beginning Hanya actually played the role of a warrior for the cause called Mary Wigman. While most of the American modern dancers were still fighting for recognition and a public in the years 1931 and 1932, Mary Wigman and her art had been acclaimed, and acclaimed on a very broad basis. Often this too created a strained atmosphere full of animosity toward Hanya as a symbol or representative rather than a person. She remembers: "I could not help seeing that there was a politeness and friendliness on the outside and a hostility on the inside."

Since it was in the area of teaching that these often irritating feelings existed, the cleansing of the atmosphere had to come in that very same area. And it happened in Bennington, Vermont.

In those days, when one spoke of "the Bennington group," one referred to Martha Graham, Doris Humphrey, Charles Weidman, and Hanya Holm, although these artist-teachers had no other relationship to one another than the fact that they had agreed to work together on the educational program as set up by the Bennington School of the Dance, a summer enterprise of Bennington College. Its aims were defined in its first prospectus in 1934.

Under the auspices of a college which includes all the arts as an essential part of its curriculum, the Bennington School is designed to bring together leaders and students interested in an impartial analysis of the important trends in the dance. The modern dance, in common with the other arts of this period, is a diversified rather than a single style. At the same time it possesses certain identifying characteristics which are common to all of its significant forms. The most advantageous plan of study is, therefore, one which reflects this diversification and, by affording comparisons, aims to reveal the essentials of modernism in the dance. The Bennington School presents contrasting approaches to technique and composition and, by giving a larger place to the related aspects of the dance, such as music, undertakes an integrated analysis of the whole structure of the art. Under this plan the student of the dance has access to the experience necessary to the formulation of a well-founded point of view.

Hanya was invited by the College to be on the advisory board of the Bennington School from the very beginning, and taught there between 1934 and 1939. John Martin, who had the chair for dance history during these summer sessions, gave the following account of the curriculum and its effect on the students in his book *America Dancing:*

> The students are given a continuous background of funda- mental technique under the direction of Martha Hill, and in ad- dition are subjected to intensive two-week courses by Martha Graham, Hanya Holm, Doris Humphrey, and Charles Weidman. Always two and sometimes three technical courses are thus going on simultaneously, and there are naturally so many conflicts of theory and opinion that any kind of specific indoctrination is totally out of the question. The immediate effect of the six weeks' session is generally one of confusion in the mind of the student, and from this he is able to extricate himself only by dint of his own effort. With the whole field thrown open to him, by way of background, he is forced to find his own solution to problems which are inevitably also his own. He is given every aid, but he has no orthodoxy to lean on, no authoritarianism to tell him what to think.

That this eclectic system sometimes caused havoc among the students is borne out by the whimsical reminiscence of Al- win Nikolais, who was a Bennington student in 1938 and 1939: "I recall a little thing that Charles used to do which illustrates the difference in techniques taught in Bennington. Martha Gra- ham was in her somewhat divine awkward state, and it is in- teresting that at this particular time the stance taught was one of feet straight forward, the hip tilted slightly backward and the shoulder a tiny bit forward, which gave an archaic appearance to the body. The position of feet and body was different from what Hanya would use so that when you went to Hanya's class you were in difficulties. One took classes with all four of them the same day and often forgot to shift gears and to create a new body for the other kind of technique. Charles indicated that with Martha you put the behind back a little, with Hanya forward, and, he said, he preferred a combination of the two and ended up by doing a bump."

But the importance of Bennington has become history and can best be judged when one considers the names of those who participated in the studies and group work: Jane Dudley, Jean Erdman, Harriette Ann Gray, Erick Hawkins, José Limón, Katherine Litz, Sophie Maslow, Sybil Shearer, Anna Sokolow — to mention a few who made a name for themselves in the forties and fifties. Among those in Hanya's group were Valerie Bettis, Eve Gentry, Louise Kloepper, and Elizabeth Waters.

Fortunately for the development of the modern dance in America, these summer sessions attracted almost everyone interested in the dance. The students came from everywhere in the States, and the student level was as varied as the methods with which the students were familiarized. A great many of the students were teachers in the physical education departments of colleges and universities. These teachers were greatly stimulated by their experiences in Bennington, they helped spread the gospel and eased the way for the companies of the big four to appear at their colleges. The artistic accomplishments of Martha Graham, Doris Humphrey, and Charles Weidman were well received on those tours, but the colleges as institutes of learning were more receptive to Hanya's lecture-demonstration performances, which offered ready-made insights into this new art form.

Besides the excitement created by the presence of the big four in Bennington, the aspiring dancers themselves were gripped by a passion for the art and by a drive to succeed. "That particular period was of great significance to the dance and to the country in general," Alwin Nikolais recalls. "This time was comparable to those great periods in the arts in which the works produced are identifiable with dynamic power and vision. There everything was action and devotion. John Martin defined the essence of such a Festival when he said that on such occasions things must occur which are new, not simply revivals of the past, that these creations must have the vitality of the contemporary and the future. The six weeks in Bennington fulfilled this purpose when one recalls the works and the many dancers they produced."

With the fever of learning and creating as high as it was among the students and with the confusion caused by the different technical approaches, the teacher-artists had to try hard to get their viewpoints across, and most of the students felt swayed toward one or another method. "To extricate himself by dint of his own effort," as John Martin described it, was more easily said and expected from them than done. Either the student remained uncertain which of the four prophets was really right, or he became partisan by choosing sides.

Neither uncertainty nor partisanship helped clear the atmosphere as far as Hanya was concerned because she brought with her the aura of the "famous" foreigner, which somehow pitted her against the other three, however much they may have differed among themselves — and there were undoubtedly three readily recognizable camps. All four were teaching a week only during the first festival at Bennington, and Hanya was eager to circumvent any mounting of ill-feelings coming from the student body. "The relationship between teacher and students has to be free of any preconceived negative attitudes from both sides. Students who come to your classes with a defensive or challenging feeling can create a bad atmosphere from which the teaching must suffer. Hostility of students is something the teacher cannot easily live down unless a miracle happens. And in the first year at Bennington such a miracle did happen."

There was a student meeting at which the students could talk freely, and during the ensuing discussion Hanya had her great chance to cleanse the atmosphere of all unclarities and uncertain feelings of why "things were the way they were." Hanya knew how to take advantage of this opportunity. She felt like Lessing's *Nathan the Wise*, who was asked by the Sultan the fateful question which of the three religions, the Jewish, the Christian, or the Mohammedan, was the right one. Was it Martha's method, the Humphrey-Weidman method, or hers? Nathan told the Sultan the parable of the wonder-working ring which a father of three sons had to leave to one and how he had copies made of the ring to be able to give one to each of his sons whom he loved and trusted with equal fervor.

Did they not all work toward the realization of one new art form with whatever technical means to achieve artistic greatness? She had learned certain things in which she believed. "This is what I have to contribute in my own way, how I have understood to walk the road to one's artistic fulfillment, and I think it is interesting to know about it for everyone here in America. That doesn't say I want to outdo anyone else, that doesn't imply that I am better than you are because there isn't such a thing, and I have never thought that way. There is no hostility or bad feeling of any sort on our side. Life is full of chances. If you can blame anyone for my being here, then blame Sol Hurok. It wasn't Mary's prompting, on the contrary she was hesitant about it, it was his doing. Now that you have your chance, make the best of it. And the best is an honest exchange of what there are of slight or greater differences in opinions and approach. Let curiosity guide you and make up your mind as to what fits best your mentality and physical frame. There shouldn't be any hard feelings. If there are, then maybe the shoe is on the other foot and things may inadvertently have been done or said which were not easy to take on either side." Hanya paused. "That brought the house down, and the students were quick in telling their teachers what had been said during the meeting. From then on I sat at the same table with Martha, Doris, Charles, and Louis."

Hanya was understood, and John Martin wrote in his book, *America Dancing*, about the Bennington group only a year later:

It was no doubt with a realization of the responsibility involved, that the faculty was selected to exemplify "the important trends in the dance." In it are found the three leading American dancers of the new school, all differing widely in method and style; a unique representative of the best modern European system, concerned far less with propagating an orthodoxy than with adapting its principles to a new environment; and the outstanding figure in the realm of dance education.

Hanya's first major work was prepared for the Bennington Festival in the summer of 1937. It was called *Trend* and was produced as the main feature in the Vermont State Armory, where the dance performances usually took place. Hanya had collaborated on this fifty-five-minute opus with Arch Lauterer, the scene designer, and the composer Wallingford Riegger.

She felt that the modern dancer must not lose himself in mere self-expression, that he must seek the creative expression of contemporary ideas and ideals. He is the spokesman for his time, as is any other serious artist. *Trend*, as well as the dance works following it which Hanya choreographed for the concert stage, was initially an emotional response to life and only afterward subjected to cerebral construction and control.

Hanya often speaks of the Faustian dichotomy of *"Zwei Seelen wohnen, ach, in meiner Brust"* — two souls, alas, dwell in my breast — which makes itself felt in the Apollonian and Dionysian in her approach to creativity. Nietzsche equated Apollo with the cult of form, and Hanya sees in the Apollonian utter simplicity, measured beauty, the indivisible whole, an art arrived at a point of rest and form-fulfillment. But she feels she would never be able to content herself with it, nor is it the Apollonian she seeks out from the beginning, being guided, as she is, by her emotional impulses. The Dionysian, the bold violence, the eternal drive to seek the new feverish dynamism, the unruly vitality, will time and again come to the fore demanding its rights. The Dionysian, as Hanya sees it, has power and urgency and, driving toward the goal of creation, may approach or even enter the gates behind which the Apollonian rules supreme.

Trend embodied both the Dionysian and Apollonian qualities. Walter Terry recalls today that in this work "her form was very apparent, much more so than in anyone else's work except in Doris Humphrey's, but both choreographers were architects of dance. Hanya was very well aware of the architecture of the human body moving in space. In *Trend* she used many pathways from the wings onto the stage, one was almost aware of them as processionals of people, or you thought of Shakespeare's actors who also had their entrances and exits and each in his turn played many parts. Hanya had lines of girls coming from the wings, from disappearance into appearance. They made an architectural form besides expressing a great deal because *Trend* spoke of our times."

Hanya must have been very much aware of the architecture of this dance — she may have thought of it as Apollonian form-fulfillment — because she had the orchestra section of the theater closed off when *Trend* was shown again the following winter at the Mecca Temple, now the New York City Center. She wanted the audience to look down on the dance to avoid any frontal view; on the contrary, to have the advantage of facing the roundness and full dimension of her architectural design. This recalls the definition of ballet in connection with the first theatrical dance, the *Ballet Comique de la Reine*, in 1581, when its choreographer Balthasar de Beaujoyeulx explained ballet as "a geometrical arrangement of several persons dancing together under a diverse harmony of many instruments."

Walter Terry pointed out that her tremendous gift for abstract design in modern dance is the equivalent of George Balanchine's in the classical ballet. And Alwin Nikolais saw it as "a magnificent symphony of movement. *Trend* was of heroic proportions using a large group. Hanya's skill in choreography was then quite evident, her German mind showing logic in her structure. In *Trend* I was deeply impressed by the visions Hanya expressed through her choreography, by the dramatic effect of small gestures done by a large group of people, gestures which in the light of space grew into great dramatic statements. The structure of her dances was very solid already in those early days, hers was always well-formed material with strong aesthetic premises. *Trend* was far more a neo-classical dance than it was modern dance in terms of the Freudian psycho-dramatic substance we normally think of as traditional modern dance. It is more difficult to describe Hanya's work than any work of the other three choreographers for the simple reason that it is difficult to describe a symphony. *Trend* was far more abstract, not necessarily with an obvious literal meaning, in short, symphonic rather than psycho-dramatic."

About the creation of her first major work Hanya told the readers of the *Magazine of Art* in March 1938 that the idea of *Trend* grew upon her, it was not a sudden inspiration:

The theme issued from life itself, rather than being built up as an intellectual construction. Impressions of years traveled a long path of development before they took shape as the theme of *Trend.*

The vision of the theme was so far expanded, so vast, that crystallization was necessary first of all. I had to eliminate and sacrifice in order to draw things together into a logical outline, to point the conception.

Then the mental image began to take shape. The motif of the whole was visionary, vital and dynamic. The form was pushed onward by timely, spatial and dynamic happenings. The visual part of the externalization resulted from experience and imagination.

The character and force of the theme itself dictated the form, the volume, shape and frame of the dance. Specifically, the dance action demanded space-creating values. Planes and levels became a necessity of the composition. Ramps of various grades, as well as steps, were essential to connect the different planes: some calling forth rhythmic dynamic space action; others long sustained sweeps. Proportions of horizontal extension in relation to vertical flight were important.

A large number of dancers was needed to carry out the weight of the action. This was not an arbitrary decision. It was a requirement inherent in the theme. Yet the performance of the dance action was by no means left entirely to mass movement. The theme calls for making various uses of the large group, of smaller groups and even individuals. There was a continuous change of weight, of volume, of linear and dimensional values.

Themes of wider significance required more mass and architectural values in concentrated or contrapuntal relation. Such numbers were *Our Daily Bread, Satiety, Cataclysm, Resurgence* and *Assurance*. I must emphasize that everything was determined by organic development, rather than intellectual decision. For example, the five episodes in the opening section grew out of the whole and led back into it.

Each episode was mainly carried by a soloist. Yet each characterization had different attention demands. In one, *Lest We Remember*, the soloist was self-sufficient. No group movement or other factor than the values of space proportions was necessary. In another, *The Effete*, the group movement was restrained, forming a sustained counterweight without action. In *From Heaven, Limited* the group was a supporting factor, and the soloist was the climactic point of the group action. In *Lucre Lunacy* the group was drawn into the soloist's activity. In the last of the episodes, *He, the Great*, the group was most prominent in reacting to the soloist. In the part I took over myself, the soloist formed the sustaining transition from a dramatic climax (*Cataclysm*), through solitude, to a new development (*The Gates Are Desolate*). In this last mentioned number the same soloist carries the *leit-motif*.

The dramatic character of *Trend* demanded a departure from the usual abstract symbolic handling of dance themes. Dance action was required rather than dance abstraction. It was imperative to call for the unification of all theatrical media. Their practical use was a thematic demand rather than a decorative decision. Theatrical setting I have already touched upon. The three-dimensional significance of space also demanded the architectural handling of light, as well as the rhythm and volume of color — in lights, costumes and the covering of the setting, the floor cloth and the cyclorama.

Hanya had been charged to present the major work of the Bennington Festival in 1937, and a major work it was, not only crowning what she had created until then, but also setting a new standard of accomplishment for group choreography. This work, performed by seven soloists and an ensemble of thirty, was different from what Bennington had seen before; it became a landmark in the then young history of the modern dance. It would have been of even greater significance for the modern dance and particularly for Hanya, had it been followed up by a sizable number of other works, but Hanya's output in the concert field remained rather limited.

In mounting *Trend* she was well supported by her comrades-in-arms, the composers Wallingford Riegger and Edgard Varèse, and particularly by the scene designer Arch Lauterer, whose principles paralleled those of Hanya and whose contributory ideas to *Trend* helped the work succeed with the unique impact it had on its audiences. Primarily, Arch Lauterer believed in movement per se and in the dance as having within it "the power to be the substratum of theater, the actual current of theater." Light and movement existed for him on the same plane, and he fought for light to be designed when the dance was being composed — and not to be put upon it as an afterthought. "The choreographer himself should know something about light and should himself conceive of it in the overall choreographic plan." And about the stage image Lauterer said that "the scenic art of dance-drama is that of creating visual images in space that add up to meaning in time. This being the case, the choreographer invents movements that reoccur as a growing theme just as in the symphonic form of music. The stage design is created also of shapes that reoccur in changing proportions and relationships throughout the time of the dance-drama." For *Trend* he built a multilevel double stage with ramps and platforms which John Martin called "the first truly modern stage setting the dance had seen."

Some of the music was composed especially by Wallingford Riegger, but Hanya was daring enough to use the avant-garde, all-percussion works — unusual in their sonority — *Ionization* and *Octandre* by Edgard Varèse to give the work the vital accents it needed. In choreographing *Trend* at Bennington Hanya had the benefit of being close to her collaborators and she could use the facilities of the college. If this opus had not been a part of her existence with which she had lived for some time, it would never have materialized as quickly as it did, within the six weeks she had at her disposal, although her step-by-step method, the slowly unfolding process in which she believes, was then as remarkable as it is today. A member of her dance company at that time, Carolyn Durand Brooks, remembers the creation of *Trend*: "Hanya was seated on a high ladder in the middle of the armory floor. It was like watching the orchestra conductor creating the music while he conducted. She would place the dancers and give them a bit of a movement to do, and then a phrase. Out of the phrase a pattern would develop. She might get two or three minutes of a dance in a morning."

John Martin wrote his report to *The New York Times* from Bennington on August 18:

> The work is on a colossal theme, the survival of society out of a state of decadence and collapse, and at present it is rather a series of sketches than a finished work . . .

After this over-all critical view, Mr. Martin went on to say:

> Miss Holm has brought a totally different approach to the matter of dance production and one that has incalculable possibilities. She has created less a large group dance than a kind of heroic choric drama in which for words are substituted movement and a kind of dramatic expressionism. In its earlier sections it is a picture of social neurosis which is extraordinary as it is compelling. After an opening movement in which men are seen as little more than automatons in a meaningless universe, there follow five episodes of smaller dimensions which comprise perhaps the finest part of the work. Here Miss Holm has exhibited a remarkable ability to employ individuals against a group, and small groups and scattered figures against larger groups for dramatic effect.
>
> The closing section, entitled "Resurgence," is set against the almost overpowering volume of Varèse's "Ionization" scored exclusively for percussion instruments. . . . The music is rhythmically of almost insuperable difficulties, but the group performs it with complete authority. Since this section is the only affirmation to be found in the whole of the long work, the total effect will be much happier when Miss Holm carries out her purpose of adding another movement to clinch her argument which is one essentially of faith and confidence.
>
> The general method of the composition is broad, sweeping and deliberate. It makes fine use of the possibilities of space and is, above all else, dramatic. The actual formal choreography is so

bent to the service of the general theme that its designs emerge chiefly in large terms and are cumulative in effect. . . .

After the first New York performance on December 29 Mr. Martin wrote:

> Hanya Holm's New York debut at the Mecca last night in a group composition of major dimensions called *Trend* served to confirm the impression made by the same work in the Bennington Festival last Summer that here is a creative talent of the first magnitude to be reckoned with. . . . [she] opens up a new vista for the production of great dance dramas. . . . It is inevitable in its development, unhurried and driving in its dramatic intensity and makes large demands upon its audience. . . . The first half of the work is a picture of progressive decadence, culminating in a magnificently built cataclysm; the remaining action is the slow and precarious return to balance. . . .
>
> Many changes have been made since the performance in Bennington. The concluding section is new, and Miss Holm's own role has been written up a bit, much to the advantage of the general effect. . . .

And his next Sunday feature said:

> What Miss Holm has done with "Trend" in the way of composition marks her as a creative choreographer of the first rank and moreover one with a rare feeling for the theatre.

With *Trend*, Hanya proved to be a genuine disciple of Mary Wigman in the universal expression of a social awareness, but she also demonstrated clearly how far she had moved away from her teacher. The work had nothing of the Germanic mysticism which so easily and hopelessly can get bogged down in obscurity. *Trend* had in its dramatic symbolism legible dramatic action; in its theatricality it was human and close to everyone's understanding. *Trend* reflected modern man's awareness of his unhappiness and his futile rebellion against it; it showed the incongruity of a world long before existentialism and the Theater of the Absurd exploited this theme. *Trend* sounded catastrophe, and more fiercely than dance ever had done before. But in its ending it avoided a facile resolution. Its prophecy was the creative power imminent in the universe, the incessant stir that shapes new forms out of chaos, the resurgence of life even where fire has burnt the last leaves of grass.

Hanya Holm proved with *Trend* that the artist is not only the last survivor of past and present, but also the prophet of the coming age.

Be as honest as you can, exclude anything that seems like
vanity. Don't follow an assumed image that is not yours.
— HANYA HOLM

The Concert Stage

HANYA had created many dances that preceded
Trend and several of importance that followed it. She continued
a tradition which she had brought with her from Germany and
which coincided with similar tendencies in the American modern dance. Often she was reproached for having choreographed
a relatively small repertory. But within less than a decade, between 1936 and 1944, she produced a good number of dances,
and she was about as prolific as the other three leading figures.
Hanya did not appear publicly with her company before 1936,
and she stopped working for the concert stage by the end of
World War II, when she could no longer financially afford to
keep her company together. It was only a short time later that
Broadway claimed her — it could not have been a more appropriate moment in her life — and Hanya and the lyric theater
found each other.

In the early thirties she had been well known for her demonstration evenings, and the demand for such concerts was still
strong long after her success with *Trend* and her establishment
as one of the major modern choreographers. She continued to
perform these demonstrations along with her dance compositions. The demonstration programs were so successful because
they appealed on a human level. Also, they were part of a visual
education of how to make up a dance, letting the material grow
virtually in front of your eyes from mere exercises to etudes to
a dance composition. Hanya brilliantly organized Mary Wig-

man material, and in the process developed it into Hanya Holm material. She gave each single dancer the chance to make substantial contributions to the demonstration so that it became a cooperative project enriched by the many personalities who danced in it.

In the beginning Hanya created short pieces. They were four- or five-minute dances which could be performed without the use of props and sets; as a matter of fact, they could be done on a bare stage of almost any size with a minimum of lighting. If the dancers were not in tights, the costumes were extremely simple. These dances were adjusted to the capacity of the company. They were the result of various inspirations, were often motivated by music or a provocative theme, or followed the challenge of a mood.

Some of these dances may have been an answer to the various problems with which she had dealt in her dance demonstrations. The demonstrations tried to re-create the exploration of principles in action. With them Hanya wanted to explain what, for instance, progress in space means and to make visually clear the strange experience of progressing in space. Some of her early creations were based on such explorations of principles. A good example is her dance *In Quiet Space*, which was on her first program, shown in 1936.

"It was a soundless treatment of the dancer's relationship to space," Hanya recalls. "Space had a language all its own, once it was my partner, then it acted like an antagonist. But whatever the space did to and with me, it was always there as a challenge, not loud and boisterous, but a calm, constant challenge, almost illusionary or imaginary."

Margaret Lloyd, dance critic of The *Christian Science Monitor*, found the visually strongest images:

> When she rises on her toes in her dance *In Quiet Space*, she is not just standing on tiptoe. The movement towers above the visible expression of it. The audience sensibly feels more than it sees. The dimensions of a movement expand in planes, travel through levels of space, and it is this extension that touches the audience

in passing. The contact is of universal, not personal significance.
The reaction is bigger than the dance, the dancer or the audience.

Undoubtedly, Hanya knew how to make space her visible
partner and opponent. It surrounded her with protective and
challenging suggestiveness. Each part of her body responded
to this challenge. In another of her articles, Margaret Lloyd
discussed a very specific detail in treating the use of the hands.
Ballet-minded reviewers chided the modern dancers in the thirties that they made too little use of their hands. Miss Lloyd
singled out a few dancers in order to counteract this argument
and mentioned particularly Hanya Holm's hands, which "are
concerned with space. They cut form into space, chiselling
space together with the movement of the whole body. They
connote the shimmer that lies in atmosphere. They suggest
the illimitable spread of space."

There was something fascinating about *In Quite Space*.
It had a lofty, limitless quality. The movement in Hanya's silver
costume often seemed unearthly as if wanting to reflect the entire cosmos. John Martin said, "*In Quiet Space* is built upon a
fine penetration into that intangible mental substance which
is sometimes called mood."

Hanya's first program began with a brief dance called *Salutation*, which achieved what it set out to do; that is, to greet
the audience. Later it was replaced by the more ambitious
Dance of Introduction, which was a very dancy dance and of
which Walter Terry wrote in 1940 that it "not only introduced
the members of the company to the audience in a duet, a quin-
tette, a solo, a trio and a full ensemble — it also served as a
dance of greeting in which movements of graciousness and joy-
ousness welcomed the audience." More than a quarter of a century later Mr. Terry fondly remembers this dance: "This prelude was a lovely work without a story that seemed to me like
a statement: 'These are my dancers, this is how we think and
feel, and this is our house, the house of dance, and this is the
way we move through this space which in the confines of the

stage is our home. This is us.' It was a statement of Hanya's technique, Hanya's attitude toward form, Hanya's girls, of Hanya herself, of very much the essence of dance as Hanya saw it."

When it was shown for the first time in New York, John Martin said that "the lilting new *Dance of Introduction* achieves a notable felicity of expression . . . has a finish and an easy charm that are captivating. There appear in it here and there unassimilated infiltrations from the academic ballet technique, which are disturbing, but on the whole its movement is free and wide and admirably controlled."

It was in the late thirties that Hanya experimented with the inclusion of certain movements borrowed from ballet technique, something that has become fully accepted three decades later. Hanya was the first choreographer in America to realize that both the modern dance and ballet could profit from taking from each other that which could enrich their own technique and concepts.* Hanya was especially harshly chided for being such an iconoclast by the editors of *Dance Observer*, who rushed to the defense of the modern dance. They neglected to see — what Hanya saw — that the modern dance was already sufficiently grown up to measure its own capacity against the centuries-old *danse d'école* and that in its rapidly developing maturity it could not help influencing the ballet as well as accepting ballet as an experienced teacher. No two art forms — however similar or different their principles may be — can exist side by side for long without penetrating each other's dogmatic walls, without coloring or discoloring some of each other's concepts.

Hanya's restless spirit never shied away from explorations, however uncomfortable the critical reaction may have been. But she also liked to return to old problems, which, she felt,

---

* In the late 1920s Kurt Jooss had suggested that the expressive modern dance be recognized as the representative dance form of the twentieth century, but that, at the same time, it should adopt some of the technical principles of the classical ballet.

were never exhausted. *Drive* was another solo which reacted to the challenge of space. It was a vibrant dance, motivated by demonic impulses. In a more superficial manner *Drive* was also described as expressing the force of modern life with the aid of drums. "It gave rise to a very dynamic dance statement," Hanya recalls, "with tremendous space consumption. Again, space was the resistance in this dance, which was a study of measuring one's capacity against resistance, and both had to be made visual by one and the same person."

Almost as an escape from such taxing tasks, Hanya turned to more playful dances which appealed to her sense of form and stylization. One was *Sarabande*, another, created somewhat later, was *Dance Sonata*, and both were helping to balance her program. *Sarabande* did not repeat the solemn and stately old dance but re-created the spirit and meaning behind its pretty dignity. When it was shown in Bennington in 1936 John Martin said that "*Sarabande*, though it suffers for poor lack of climax, is technically beautiful and full of delicate comment." In such dances Hanya could give forceful expression to her sense of architectural form, but she could also give free reign to the flow of lyricism. It was on such occasions that Margaret Lloyd was moved to state that Hanya was "gentle as a well-tempered clavichord."

Dance Sonata interested her because the problems involved brought her back to her early music training. She had to translate music into dance as in her days with Dalcroze, to transpose the four sonata movements into four mood pieces; she had to probe how dance forms would best fit their musical shape. *Dance Sonata*, to Harrison Kerr's music, was referred to by George Beiswanger in the April 1939 issue of *Theatre Arts Monthly*:

> In her work one can find rhythms that are dramatically conceived, melodies in movement that take the breath away, and a stage that isn't a stage at all but the rallying ground of the openness which surrounds it, a centre towards which dancers spring but from which they also continually fly. Movement . . . is the dramatic force out of which her dance is generated.

Dance in Two Parts, to a score by Wallingford Riegger, was a group dance with a strong social comment. It was inspired by some of the riots which sporadically took place before America entered World War II. The first section, "A Cry Rises in the Land," mirrored the restlessness of the masses, their contained fury, a volcanolike trembling running through their bodies; while the second part, "Toward New Destinies," reflected an outlook of promise, or some hope, although without finding a positive ending.

There were always different reasons and motivations which prompted the creation of these dances. One was Hanya's fascination with the strange sensations remembered from her nightly walks through the silent streets of New York. "I imagined such a street, so very much alive with all the hustle and bustle of daytime traffic, and then suddenly darkness and silence would envelop the city and become menacing, filled with the lure of dangers; the strange behavior of the people moving through this silence and darkness would add a sinister feeling to the entire atmosphere."

The result was *City Nocturne*. John Martin, who reviewed it in Bennington in the summer of 1936, called it "an excellent dance, original in its design, pungent in its comment and beautifully danced to a first-rate musical setting by Wallingford Riegger. Its suggestion of the jazz motif of metropolitan night life and its employment of strange grotesqueries of movement add to the gay note of its satire." *City Nocturne*, also described by Margaret Lloyd as "iridescent with bumpy, jerky movements and bright with satire," was a poetic presentation of cold, factual images, of fear and ugliness and the ceaseless energy of a large city.

In 1936, when Hanya presented her group for the first time and toured extensively with her first program, she also included a rather humorous number about which Margaret Lloyd wrote:

In her *Four Chromatic Eccentricities* the first part is intentionally overflowing with undisciplined energy and emotion; the second, as she describes it, is "catching the impossible," now frivolous, now indolent; the third is yearning and self-pity — self-dramatization without any real feeling; and the fourth crazily ridiculous, chasing one's own tail, dissipating all one's resources. All exaggerate familiar traits to the point of incongruity. Humor in movement unmasking human frailties by reducing them to absurdity. . . . In none of these dances does Hanya Holm use movement as description. Always it is the essence of experiences extracted and phrased in the motor medium. She is averse to extraneous ornament, to overrefined detail.

John Martin went a step further and characterized the *Four Chromatic Eccentricities* as a completely nonsensical study in low comedy, but he also stressed that Hanya achieved in this creation the rare distinction of being funny without departing for an instant from the dimensions of pure movement. Whenever Hanya tried her hand at humor, even if she did not mind placing herself in the area of low comedy, as Mr. Martin thought, she always revealed her consummate feeling for the motor phrase, her masterly sense of form. In this dance Hanya was interested in drawing character sketches and giving satirical impressions of different personality types by making a small step beyond common logic. "I had my fun with it," she says, and what she achieved was fun for the audience, which always enjoys eccentricities.

This first program closed with two dances in which the entire group was involved in an abandon of motor movement, stamping, leaping, and whirling. *Primitive Rhythm* was a perfect wedding of primitive music and movement. The unusually rousing effect was obtained by the thumping of hands and feet on the floor in the excitement of the dance to supplement piano and percussive instruments. The rhythmic, almost savage, surge which reflected the joy of the dancers in being children of nature had a contagious quality about it. The idea was one of a *perpetuum mobile*, with the whole tightly knit group treading continuously, with arms thrust out like rhythmic accents, finally turning into a state of ecstatic exuberance.

Primitive Rhythm led to *Festive Rhythm*, with overtones of a joyous celebration, a finale with the rich colors of a ritual. In summing up Hanya's first program John Martin said in one of his reviews that there is "a building of design in terms of sequential movement . . . logical with an inherent motor logic" and that her style is "naturally delicate and intimate . . . she knows the stuff of movement as if by instinct."

Hanya's first program preceding *Trend* made it quite clear that here was a modern dancer whose choreography was a vital contribution to the new movement. It was very different from anything that Martha Graham, Doris Humphrey, Charles Weidman, and Helen Tamiris did. The technique did not deny its Mary Wigman origin, but by then it had changed into a very personal concept as Hanya had adjusted to the new environment. It had the stamp of Hanya's personality, or, as Walter Terry said, "her dancing spoke with an American accent."

No serious critic doubted that out of her American experiences, Hanya had composed several dances. Moreover, everyone recognized that her company was extremely well trained. In February 1941 Walter Terry said in his column: "Hanya Holm and her girls were always the most lyric of the moderns. While the feminine contingent of other modern dance companies usually resembled a gang of sexless automatons, Miss Holm's girls inevitably danced with feminine grace and charm." More than twenty-five years later Mr. Terry recalled how very much he was impressed by her group. "I still remember that her dancers had more personality than the dancers in any of the other ensembles, they were most feminine dancers. Louise Kloepper was one of the most exciting girls, and then there were Valerie Bettis and Eve Gentry. I loved Hanya's company because of the difference and femininity. At that period she was unique."

She was also unique in not performing in New York first, but in taking her company to Colorado and Bennington, later to Chicago and other cities. It was only with *Trend* that she began her New York performances. From her dance demonstrations, she had acquainted an audience with her style and technique.

When Hanya came to Chicago in February 1937 she had to give one of her demonstrations at Thorne Hall, followed by her dance program at the Auditorium Theatre. John Martin had given a lecture a few days previously at Thorne Hall, outlining the reasons for people's difficulty in understanding the modern dance. He explained that, first of all, we expect to have the music "interpreted"; second, that we have literary minds and assume that every movement must "mean" something; third, that we think dancers are exponents of self-expression and showing off; and fourth, that "beauty" has been considered the aim of art, whereas interest is more important. But Hanya was still pioneering and was often misunderstood or at least not appreciated by some of the reviewers. Claudia Cassidy, who three years later was to praise Hanya as a beautiful and exciting dancer-choreographer, wrote at that time in the *Chicago Journal of Commerce:*

> Less clear to me is the reason for dancing as exemplified by Hanya Holm and her group at the Auditorium. Stemming from the Wigman school, their work involves the squatting posture which to me is the ugliest sight in the dance world. Why an audience should pay to watch women in dull costumes leap about a stage in fruitless exercise is something beyond my ken. What I saw of the program was choreographically dull, even "Primitive Rhythm," which began in centrifugal promise, meandering off into just jumping.

Ann Barzel, reporting from Chicago for *Dance Magazine,* found Hanya's demonstrations "thoroughly enjoyable" and thought that the most appreciated dances of the program were the group numbers *City Nocturne* and *Primitive Rhythm* as well as *Festival Rhythm.* Hanya's group was admirably disciplined and performed well, she felt. Cecil Smith, writing in the *Chicago Daily Tribune,* thought that:

> Miss Holm's program served first and foremost to scotch the widespread, if absurd, impression that modern dancing does

not require much technique. Even the members of the Monte Carlo Ballet [then the most popular ballet company in America] do not achieve greater suppleness or sureness of body control than the seven girls who form the Holm group. Louise Kloepper, to name only one, can leap with an elevation and grace which even Leonide Massine and Paul Petroff could not surpass without difficulty. All the girls in the group repeatedly accomplished technical feats of great virtuosity in that skillful manner which makes them look perfectly easy.

Hanya realizes that her first group was a perfect instrument in her hands. It was not a company on a salary, no one was hired. Everyone's time and energy was voluntarily contributed toward a common goal. Whatever there was to be done was recognized by everyone as a communal task. Everything worked very smoothly in a cooperative spirit. It was an ideal condition under which to work. Hanya's first five years in America were spent that way, with daily work, with daily preparation for the future. She could use time in a lavish manner, could branch out in bold experimentation because her dancers were thoroughly trained in and raised with discussions and experiments. Hanya liked to bring up new ideas and problems all the time, to move on bystreets which only seemingly led away from the main line of thinking and finally led back to it, enriching it with new experiences. But such a process needs time and patience, willingness to sacrifice, and understanding beyond the call of duty, an almost blind belief in what one does. "It was marvelous to work with them," Hanya says. "My dancers were only dominated by the spirit of 'Let us get together and do something together.' The dancers were prepared in their spatial understanding, no movement was forced upon them. If I wanted to do something without music, for instance, and spelled it out in terms of dynamics as a succession, the girls got it without doing it twice. I could paint in space with them. These were ideal circumstances under which I could work in those years."

The world went through cataclysmic events between 1938 and 1944, and Hanya's work reflected the seriousness of the times. She has never believed that art should become a champion for any political cause, right or left, nor that dancing could easily be an instrument with which to take up the fight for any pro or con and here or there. But the upheavals went beyond mere political expression, they brought about war, the mass murder of minorities, the slaughter and exile of the innocent. The artist cannot fail to be of this world and his time; he may not necessarily take sides, but he must be on the side of humanity.

The world problems were manifold, and Hanya's sensibilities were attuned to them in varied manner. *Dance of Work and Play* was a comment on work as an essential part of man's being. Alfred Frankenstein, writing in the *San Francisco Chronicle* in November 1938, was impressed by it as "largely an abstract work, but it derived much expressive meaning from its dramatic theme, which dealt with labor as a thing both of joy and sorrow." It was a suite in six parts with music by Norman Lloyd.

Formal unity of the various parts was attained through the device of having Hanya introduce each theme, which was later developed by her group. Each of the sections showed a different approach to the subject of work and play, only to be reconciled in the finale, called "Synthesis." First, Hanya presented "The Empty-Handed," who have nothing to give and who receive nothing for their sterile work. Then there were those "Driven," who moved with frenzied gestures through their dry and tedious labors. The mechanical, chained movements as well as their rigidity bespoke our mechanized civilization. The pillars formed by three figures in the foreground were a dramatic and novel use of space design. Also, there was the "Solitary," who tried to find a solution on his own. Then the dance rose to an exciting and joyous climax in "Communal" and "Synthesis," when all moved together in a single strong line toward an ultimate goal. The ending seemed to be a symphony of motion with many falls in perfect unison.

Henry Gilfond of the *Dance Observer* put thumbs down on

this work by saying that "mood rather than opinion is the essence of the dance, an impressionistic work that would reveal the essence of the different stages represented by the different titles of the sections. But the fundamental forces underlying the various phases of the work are not considered and the dance resultingly floats away from whatever base it might rest on." Margaret Lloyd was of a different opinion, writing that it "hit the heart and reached the understanding without program notes and only a hasty glance at subtitles. It was organic, eloquent — design irradiated by idea. Miss Holm, dancing with a new openness and freedom, introduced and concluded each theme in a solo statement. Her concert group, with accustomed proficiency, worked them out."

Hanya remembers that "what interested me in this dance was not only the action but the situation of human progress. I proceeded from the premise that when we play we work, when we work we play. Of course, playing was not something frivolous or flippant to me but was seen as enjoyment and satisfaction like work that is neither dragging nor depressing. I wanted to investigate where the difference was between work and play. It was broken down to communal and personal experiences because even an isolated person like a hermit sitting all by himself in his monastery cell is working. I used some compositional devices which interested me very much. For instance, in one of the communal scenes I placed three figures between audience and dancers, and used them as space design, so to speak, instead of props. The audience had to look past these three figures standing there like dark silhouettes, in no way emotionally connected with the dancers moving in bright light. These figures were set pieces, limitations to the eye, and had the characteristics of dancers utterly dehumanized."

Turning to humor again, Hanya created a much approved and loudly applauded work, *Metropolitan Daily*. It was a satire on newspapers. She dealt with each section separately, selecting some that seemed to translate more easily into dance terms:

foreign news, finances, the comics, the society page, the scandal sheet, want ads, and the sports page. Biting wit alternated with broad humor. Walter Terry wrote in the *New York Herald Tribune* in December 1938 that "it was slapstick, it was fun, it was theatrically entertaining. . . . The acrobatically attained pyramid [in the 'sports section'] was the perfect ending for this excellent work. In spite of failings, the dance of Hanya Holm is one of the high spots in the contemporary dance of America."

The previous month, when Hanya was with her group in San Francisco, Alfred Frankenstein wrote in the *Chronicle:* "It was subtly organized in true choreographic movement, and the resource of invention and composition in the final sports movement was a marvel to behold." After having seen *Metropolitan Daily* and *Dance of Work and Play*, Cecil Smith was moved to exclaim in the *Chicago Daily Tribune:* "Miss Holm has always been the finest choreographer among modern dancers, and now that she is gaining a theater sense Martha Graham will do well to look to her laurels."

In 1939 Hanya created *Tragic Exodus* and shortly afterwards *They Too Are Exiles*. Both works were inspired by the catastrophic events that had overcome mankind in those days. The frightening spectre of thousands of people impelled to flee Hitler Germany, the forced migration to escape death in a concentration camp, was behind *Tragic Exodus*. The Spanish Civil War, with the people facing and fighting the power of dictatorship and finally having to live with the fear of the whip, led to the creation of *They Too Are Exiles*. But neither work shows a direct reference to the actual political happenings. Hanya did not intend to take sides in an ideological struggle. What interested her were the human motivations of power and the human suffering caused by it; the question of what keeps mankind restless, what creates the turmoil in our thinking; the forces of evil that were behind one upheaval and crept into the other. Thus, the second work was a second installment, seen from another angle, another viewpoint. It was even less specific, was broader and more remote from reality in its human and artistic aspects than the first dance comment on the times. In order to make this unmistakably clear a footnote in the program said that "it is not the choreographer's desire to represent specific countries." It was as if Hanya wanted to state that it happened there, but that it can happen here or anywhere as well.

Tragic Exodus was immediately recognized as an incisive work. In July 1939 the annual award of *Dance Magazine* went to Hanya for this group composition with the dedication: "*Tragic Exodus* is of uniform excellence as a dance, it has great emotional appeal and it is of topical significance . . ."

They Too Are Exiles juxtaposed the figure of the Possessor and the people living under his reign. This work showed through various movements the curtailment of the freedom of different folk groups under the whip of the Possessor. Hanya, wearing a green and black costume designed to represent dignity and power, played the part of the Possessor, a force cruelly unleashed or a system but not any particular individual. The people and their desires for a peaceful existence were characterized by folk dances of Slavic, Latin, and Teutonic origin. The appearance of the Possessor stamped out their gaiety and paralyzed with fear their daily lives. In the end the Possessor destroyed himself and his country.

The critiques were less favorable about this work than *Tragic Exodus*. Only Alfred Frankenstein came out in favor of it when he wrote that both ballets "dealt with some of the big questions that cloud man's minds today." He thought that *They Too Are Exiles* "was perhaps the more impressive piece. It was an almost balletic composition with episodes of folk dance and other choreographic symbols of peaceable pursuits destroyed and regimented by a sinister figure compounded of all the despots who have ruled by fear."

It was mainly this figure as portrayed by Hanya which ran into difficulties with the critics. The general consensus was that for all the energy she put into her Borgia-like, demonic part, her very style did not permit of such satanic portraiture as the composite of dictatorship. In January 1940 John Martin called it a companion piece to the previous season's *Tragic Exodus:*

> Where the earlier work dealt with people driven from their native land by political persecution, the new composition treats of those who are left at home with no means of escape from a life that "has dwindled to a frightened whisper in the dark." It consists essentially of a series of group dances based on folk themes from various sources, with the sinister figure of the Possessor interfering and destroying the pattern in every case.
>
> The dances themselves are charmingly composed, but the role of the antagonist leaves something to be desired. Miss Holm is far too gentle and ingratiating a personality to bring conviction to [this] character. Actually, the work would stand alone and gain considerably in the elimination of obviousness if this role were written out altogether.

Whoever spoke of the theater as an impure art form, to which many minds and bodies contribute their share for better or worse, could not have found a better example than *The Golden Fleece* in order to prove how easily something can go wrong. To begin with, it was the idea of the surrealist painter Kurt Seligmann to create a ballet with strong surrealistic overtones about "An Alchemistic Fantasy," as the subtitle proclaimed. Kurt Seligmann also wrote the program note, which seemed involved and mystified the reader rather than enlightening him. The work had to do with the prophetic dream of a fourteenth-century alchemist named Nicolas Flamel, and seven stages in the process of turning base metals into gold. Hermes Trismegistus — the Egyptian moon god credited with powers of alchemy and magic — as well as Jason and the mythological story of the Golden Fleece were interwoven in the idea basic to his work, although they did not appear on stage.

What did appear on stage were dancers who were elaborately costumed in the most fantastic way possible as the allegorical figures they represented. The costumes, designed by Seligmann, were stunning at first sight and never tired the eye. In the first part of the composition all the dancers — male or female — were costumed in reddish-brown tights. Egg cups

5. (a) & (b) *Trend.*

6. "Want Ads," *Metropolitan Daily*: Hanya Holm, Louise Kloepper.

7. (a) *Tragic Exodus:* Hanya Holm and Company. (b) *Festive Rhythm:* Hanya Holm and Company.

8. *The Golden Fleece:* Louise Kloepper, Kipp Kiernan.

were sitting on their heads. The long golden hair was of course the Golden Fleece. The eggs in the cups were symbolic of life.

The second part of the dance featured clearly defined characters who expressed a general philosophy of life in a fantastic variety of thoughts through movement. The Inner Eye, for instance, was a character representing an alchemist who also had the full responsibility of the drama's action. Raven-Phoenix was a bird that appeared first as a raven which pecks and symbolizes disintegration; then it appears as phoenix or rebirth. Saturn was a heavy fellow displaying weight. Cosmic Oven was fire or sun, Bushel of Wings symbolized air, Fruit Bearing Tree stood for everything growing, Self Grinding Mill was indicative of the earth, and the Serpent symbolized many things such as wisdom and guardian. The entire work was a colorful fantasy of the behavior of each symbolic character and of the relationship of the characters toward each other. The symbolism was kept alive throughout the composition. To give an example: Cosmic Oven, Water, and the Self Grinding Mill danced a trio in unison displaying the unity of sun, water, and earth.

The Golden Fleece was premiered at the Mansfield Theatre on March 17, 1941. Walter Terry dismissed this work with the remark that the costumes of Kurt Seligmann were fantastic to an extreme but that the dancing failed to match their inventiveness and was much too delicate and noncommittal instead of being equally strong and grotesque. John Martin had taken the trouble to see some rehearsals before opening night and was therefore the only critic able to judge the choreographic intention as originally planned, and the effect of the costumes on Hanya's movements. He expressed his judgment by saying:

> Here for the first time the modern dance turned outside its usual pursuits to investigate the possibilities of an alliance with surrealism . . . Kurt Seligmann devised the theme of the work and designed its constumes . . . which monopolize the attention.
>
> Having seen the work in rehearsal, both with and without the costumes, one is able to testify that its choreography has form and flow, that its movements are intrinsically interesting

and its designs alive and frequently beautiful. What is wrong is the basic concept that makes movement secondary to costume.

It may have been a mistake to allow a related art to lead the way for the dance, but as soon as Hanya became interested in the challenge which the basic idea offered, the mistake and its consequences were unavoidable. It was impossible to tell the alchemist story through movements, such as quicksilver turning into gold, particularly when the heavy costuming was a serious impediment to movement. Moreover, such a strange symbolic work should have had no program notes at all, leaving everything to the imagination of the audience; or it should have delineated the happenings on stage in a legible libretto to facilitate the understanding of the average spectator.

Hanya thought that a libretto would have been helpful. Also, she felt, this dance should have been done allegorically from the beginning to the end. Then the work would have turned into such extreme stylization that a minimum of movement might have been justified with regard to the visually unusual costumes. "If we had had the costumes from the very beginning, it would have been a different matter. But the costumes were the last thing to be ready. We rehearsed to the very end without them. Much of the movement was born out of the spirit of alchemy and of the various elements we dealt with. Dynamically, it came close to what we had visualized. For instance, Louise Kloepper, who danced the bird Phoenix, had those characteristic pecking movements, but the moment she put on her mask she fell flat on her nose. The big hat had too much weight. The masks also limited the dancers' vision. These things had to be taken into account in the last minute with the result that only half the choreography got on stage. I quite agree with my critics that the costumes, which were of a high calibre, killed the dance. We made those costumes ourselves, every stitch was done in our studio on 11th Street, everything was constructed with hammer and nails and wire. Everything was hand-made. I dyed the costumes, and I remember in dyeing the costume for Sulphur, that huge male figure, the analine dye had to be squeezed in with a roller, and when I tried to lift the costume, full of water as it was, I injured my back. I had to perform the entire dance of Quicksilver with a corset on. But it was interesting to work with the surrealist principles which Kurt Seligmann represented. We often fought over certain ideas because in painting you can do so many things which you can't do in dancing, the body is different from a canvas or from sculptured material."

The Golden Fleece was a failure. It had been hard work. Hanya had injured her back. "It was a wonderful challenge," she says, "I would not have liked to miss it, not for anything in the world."

> To be simple is the most difficult thing to achieve.
> — Hanya Holm

Colorado Springs

All those who have seen Hanya in action in New York and in Colorado Springs agree that she is a different person out West. The lighter, thinner mountain air, the closeness to nature, the freedom of space, and the relaxed manner of the people in the West do something to her. To have escaped the confinement and the nervous pace of the city makes another person of her.

Without denying the seriousness of the business for which she has gone to Colorado Springs every summer since 1941, she can recapture the innocence and joy of a child. Whenever her time permits, usually before the courses begin or after they end, she will make excursions in the mountains. Having gone to Colorado Springs summer after summer for more than a quarter of a century, she has been accepted as a native. She is well known and knows her way around. She has many friends there in and outside of the College. She has helped shape the profile of the place. Colorado College and Colorado Springs are well aware of it; and, since raising a monument to her now would be in bad taste, the College did the next best thing and conferred on her an honorary Doctor of Fine Arts degree in 1960.

Hanya loves to go for long walks along the Monument River or the various avenues with their huge shady trees, and she can enjoy looking at every flower, every branch on her way. On certain afternoons one can see her sitting under a tree with a number of her students. Then teaching continues informally on the green. "Even though it is all frolicsome and entertaining," says Dr. Juana de Laban, who spent a few summers with Hanya at Colorado College, "she scrutinizes you and observes very carefully what you are attempting to do while you improvise or ask her questions about certain movement problems. There were moments out on the lawn when Hanya would talk about her viewpoints, her philosophy in relation to the art of the dance, how it manifests itself in its many media and at which point we can actually say a certain dance has become an art. It is often difficult for some of the young people to infer the relationships she is trying to get across. Nevertheless, these sessions in the afternoon are favored by the students. The formality of the classroom hampers some interchange, these more informal meetings on the green loosen up spirit and body, and it is often there that some of the ideas jell."

Don Redlich, who has also been with Hanya in Colorado for many summers, stresses that he has learned the most from her there, where she is far more relaxed and herself than in her urban existence. "There," he remarks, "you feel isolated, but, at the same time, you can concentrate on what you are doing, you understand much better what she is getting at, everything is there as if in a capsule and makes sense. Studying technique in New York with her just becomes the technique, something codified, something to be done, while the same in Colorado seems to have a bigger dimension."

Before the summer of 1941, when she became associated with Colorado College as the director of the dance summer sessions, Colorado and Hanya were no strangers. She had often been there previously, teaching or with her group, thus becoming thoroughly familiar with its people and places, its valleys and mountains, but also familiarizing the Coloradans interested in the arts with her ideas and craftsmanship. Her association with Colorado goes back to the early thirties when the modern dance was not yet generally accepted. It was in 1933 that Hanya was invited to teach in Colorado at the Perry-Mansfield school in Steamboat Springs. Three years later, she formed her own dance company. Mrs. Thomas Patterson-Campbell, head of Pro Musica in Denver, was instrumental in bringing Hanya and her company for its first recitals to Colorado. Hanya still remembers them as "smash successes." About her first major tour, in the winter of 1936, *Theatre Arts Monthly* reported in its February issue of 1937:

> A six-day tour to Colorado made recently by Hanya Holm and her group under the auspices of the Denver Chapter of Pro Musica . . . those six days contained a solid program of concerts, lectures, demonstrations, lessons and discussions at the theatres, colleges and clubs to capacity audiences everywhere. The note referring to the concert at the Broadway Theatre in Denver says of the audience of a thousand people, "This was capacity; the top balcony was open for the first time in many years and not only was that filled but standing room also was sold." In Colorado Springs an afternoon and evening performance both recorded capacity audiences, and at Boulder the evening concert had an audience of two thousand.

Martha Wilcox, who was a dance instructor at Colorado College, talked Hanya into teaching in Colorado Springs during the summer months. It did not take much coaxing since, as Hanya told interviewers in 1965: "I am attracted to the West. I love the clear skies, the light, dry air, the wide open spaces and the majestic mountains, which are wonderful stimulants in contrast to the drive and nervousness of the big city."

Hanya designed a dance program for such a summer session, and in 1941 a six-week course was set up. "After that we experimented a good bit," Hanya remembers. "We tried courses that ran through six weeks, eight and ten weeks." But soon an eight-week session was considered the best setup for the students and since then has been adhered to regularly. The curriculum consists of technique, theory, composition, music for dance, Labanotation, and dance pedagogy. Hanya has taught most of the technique, theory, and composition classes, but she has always been assisted by several teachers of her choice. Later she relinquished some of the burden of teaching to her assistants, but, as all teachers agree, she has a very firm grip on the way the teaching is conducted. She would see to it that beyond the individuality of the teacher her basic concepts are conveyed properly to each class and that no alien information contaminates the proven principles.

Her assistants also have helped her with the informal dance recitals which always concluded the eight-week sessions and consisted of dance works mostly choreographed by her students. Of course, some of the works presented were composed by her staff and, particularly during the first twelve years, by herself. During the summer sessions, other festive events also took place, and in the beginning she sometimes shared the program with the drama department, which put on such works — or excerpts from them — as Maxwell Anderson's *Barefoot in Athens* and Christopher Fry's *A Phoenix Too Frequent* and *The Lady's Not for Burning*. The department of music participated in these programs from time to time with instrumental works or pieces for *a capella* chorus.

But essentially it always was a dance program, and through the years it was under Hanya's sole direction. She was very careful to avoid the label of a finished production. To this very day these performances are to her workshop productions which have been variously called "Summer Dance Demonstrations," "Summer Students Workshop in Dance," "An Informal Dance Recital," or simply "Workshop."

Hanya supervises the progress of each dance composition whoever may author it, but she would often ask her assistants to help clean up a work done by less experienced students after she had seen it in its raw draft and given her advice. During the first few years she invited several well-known dancers — most of whom she had worked with in New York — to come to Colorado Springs to appear with her in the final production. They would also function as teachers during these sessions and work with the student body on a new creation. In the main, however, Hanya has always relied on the students and stimulated them to create their own dances, whether on the basis of a demonstration or a choreographic concept. Some of her students have become well-known dancers, and they have returned to take classes, to teach, and to choreograph during these summer sessions. Among them were Valerie Bettis, Marc Breaux, Elizabeth Harris, Ray Harrison, Nancy McKnight Hauser, Dorothy Jarnac, Murray Louis, Molly Lynn, Michael Maule, Alwin Nikolais, Don Redlich, and Glen Tetley.

Those advanced dancers and choreographers have been more than welcomed by Hanya. "It is to their credit," she says, "that they feel the need to return and expose themselves to further criticism and new stimulation to continue their own work. At Colorado College facilities are excellent and distractions minimal. This forces the participants to a greater insight and leads them to a judgment of values. I try to guide them to be able to exercise a more precise evaluation of their own thinking and their progress. Proof of the students' development is indicated by their resulting independent work and the greater respect and security of their own ideas. My intent to enlarge their experience and reveal new horizons bears fruit in their own creative statements in their chosen profession."

Only in the 1940s when Hanya did all the choreography and also appeared in the end-term programs as a featured dancer were these evenings presented by Colorado College as a "Hanya Holm Dance Concert." In the early forties her assistant was Martha Wilcox; later they were Alwin Nikolais, Molly Lynn, and Oliver Kostock. The composers and pianists with whom Hanya has worked most often over the years are Roy Harris, Freda Miller, John Colman, and Leonard Taffs.

"For four years I went to Colorado," Alwin Nikolais states, "the first year primarily as a dancer and after that as a teacher. I shared teaching the classes with Hanya and sat next to her as her assistant when she choreographed for the final productions. Frequently she gave me chores to do which were mainly cleaning-up businesses, stabilizing some of the choreography, but this opportunity afforded me a better chance to see the way she structured things and the care with which she proceeded in her choreography."

Some of Hanya's more important creations for the concert
stage had their origin in these summer sessions. The first new
dance was staged the very first year. At that time she still had
her company, whose members took part in the three performances of the festival in August. The program featured *Dance of
Introduction, Metropolitan Daily,* and the world premiere, *From
This Earth.* The *Colorado Springs Gazette Telegraph* reported:

> Before a gala audience, a large and noteworthy gathering, Hanya
> Holm wrote history for Colorado Springs last night at the Fine
> Arts Center. For the first time in the annals of the city a world
> premiere took place, and that not the work of one eminent art-
> ist but of two: Hanya Holm, distinguished exponent of the con-
> temporary dance, and Roy Harris, recognized leader among
> present day American composers.

Roy Harris not only wrote the score, he also came up with
a story outline which was based on the life of the Pennsylvania
miners. That the basic idea was not Hanya's may have been a
handicap. John Martin, in his rather complimentary review —
when this dance was shown in New York the following season
— said that "its virtues are occasionally hidden under a difficult semi-literalism." He commented on the opening number,
"Dawn — Mother's Lullaby," "which is so unsentimental and
unadorned that its title assumes an ironic color that was perhaps not intended. Miss Holm has never danced more elo-
quently or with greater command of movement."

It was a powerful opening of compassion and brooding concern. Hanya wore an enormously wide skirt, "with which I
could do many things," she recalls, "cradling and hiding. This
number was based on the function of the costume." It was the
only solo among five sections dealing with the ages of man in
the form of a suite with a recapitulation in its final number,
called "Dusk — Retrospection," that marked the unity of the
whole.

The second section, "Childhood," pictured the period of the
youthful playing of games. It may have suffered, as Martin puts
it, "from the inevitable difficulty of making grown people convincing when they attempt to be children in any literal way."

The third part dealt with love, courtship, marriage, and festivities; it was conceived with great individuality and managed to project a curiously muted sense of gaiety. The fourth section, "Work — Treadmill and Exhaustion," was the most dramatic part and, with three men and one child worker chained to the treadmill, gave a biting social comment. During the finale the same dark clouds hung over the people with the hopelessness of feeling that man's only reward is mere survival. John Martin wrote that *From This Earth* "showed itself to be a distinguished composition, deeply felt, skillfully realized, and not easy to put out of one's mind."

During the second summer session in Colorado Hanya began to experiment with dance to the spoken word, which especially interested her. The poetic immortalization of small town life in Edgar Lee Master's *Spoon River Anthology* intrigued her. Having been close to small town life in the West, she felt a kinship with the people of the Spoon River in Illinois and came up with the idea of *Namesake*. She called it "A Theatre Dance" and selected several persons from the anthology, who, in the costumes of the period, danced the story of their lives to the poem, which was recited. Roy Harris composed the music for this dance. Scenario and design were created by Arch Lauterer, whose S-shaped white wall in the rear covered two-thirds of the stage. There were no attempts made to create the illusion of a cemetery or tombstones, as might have been justified by the poems. The mood and the magic of the atmosphere had to come from the dancers supported by suggestive lighting. "For me," Hanya says, "it was a new experience, another facet of the dance with a great deal of miming. Already at that time I felt compelled to move into other directions, toward a lyric dance theater."

In the following year, 1943, she returned to folk material when she choreographed *Suite of Four Dances* based on American folk songs with the music arranged by Roy Harris. Orchestra and chorus accompanied the dances. But that year the more ambitious creation was Hanya's *Orestes and the Furies*, which related in dance form the mental torment of a man who has killed his mother. Hanya stresses, "It was not created as a modern comment on our own Orestes problems, the torture of our conscience by whatever furies we may face nowadays. There was more of a Greek mood about it. I tried to catch the frightening aspects of man's tortured conscience through the centuries, something timeless, nevertheless very human. But it did not quite satisfy me from a purely choreographic viewpoint."

When this work was shown at the Washington Irving High School in New York the following season, it was not well received by the press. Edwin Denby wrote: "It looked to me like a graduation event put on by the girls' physical education department; posture work, intermediate and advanced, neatly and seriously performed." However, Mr. Denby liked the *Suite of Four Dances*, "built on mild variations of speed and rearrangements of small groups [it] was easy, clean and simple. A duet in it was charmingly danced by Joan Palmer and Paul Sweeney, two dancers with a native instinct for the theater; and after that the rest of the number went off very well indeed. It would please on any program."

What Dreams May Come was the major feature on the 1944 summer program. This dance came in the wake of the psychological dance-dramas treated by Humphrey, Weidman, and Graham, and, particularly at that time, by the younger generation. Hanya used a décor of Freudian significance. It was composed of three huge triangles pointed toward the audience. The set was part of the choreography. It was movable, and the triangles could open and display the dancers who were inside. The triangles themselves were conceived as stage area, and the other space of the stage was filled at certain times with non-moving dancers playing spectators. The overlapping stage images gave the idea of a dance within a dance. "All was fantasy and the illogical happenings of our dream world," she remembers. "At first, bright and dark and shadowy refractions of the dreamer's personality danced through her dreaming.

Then the action moved into the subliminal, and, as in the later dances of the absurd, whatever happened made little sense although it was heavy with meaning. At one point, for instance, somebody pinned a medal on me, then the wishful dream of the redeemer became nightmarish reality, with the crowd lifting me up and liberating me. These were dream sequences of unrelated characters. I danced the dream, and at the end I went right back into the womb, so to speak, I was sucked into the walls which closed, and then the dream ended."

About that time another dream had come to an end for Hanya. With the growing financial demands made on her to keep her company afloat, she finally had to dissolve it. From then on, having no company in New York, she had no outlets for her choreographic skills except in Colorado, where her organizing genius and her desire to let her teachers and students try their hands at choreography came to the fore. Hanya created fewer and fewer dances for the concert stage with the years, particularly after 1948, when her interest in the lyric theater coincided with her first successes on Broadway.

The dissolution of her company also terminated her career as a dancer. She continued to appear on stage for a few more years during the final workshop productions in Colorado Springs, "as necessitated on certain occasions," as she puts it. Hanya was still seen on stage in *Xochipili* in the summer of 1948, but in the following year when she staged Stravinsky's *History of a Soldier* at Colorado Springs Fine Arts Center, she found in Mildred Kaeser a young dancer whom she could trust with the role of the Princess, the part that had started Hanya's own dancing career. Miss Kaeser, who also re-created this role at the Aspen Festival in 1954, often took over parts which Hanya might have had to dance. Hanya had never had to make the vital decision — one which is a crucial moment in the life of a dancer — when to stop her dancing career. She simply glided out of it.

Hanya danced the solo, "Alone," in her creation of *Win-*

dows, in 1946. The score was by Freda Miller, who for years was her faithful accompanist. You looked through *Windows* into the life of various people. The opening and closing scenes took place in an office. All dancers sat in front of imaginary typewriters acting as imaginary typists, symbolizing the mechanization of our daily existence. This was underlined by the masks the dancers were wearing. When they left the office they took off their masks, hanging them on a rack from which they took them to put them on again in the final scene. "These people were conformists on their jobs, but the minute they left the office, they snapped out of being mechanized humans. They all had their life experiences, their dramatic fantasies. My solo was a mood piece characterized by the idea that no one was coming into my life to share with me the hours that really matter."

Xochipili (1948) was inspired by the Mexican painter Ricardo Martínez, who designed the set and costumes for this dance in three scenes. Percussion accompaniment and a recording of a composition by Carlos Chávez using ancient Aztec instruments went with this stylized dance about the recurring cycle of the rise and fall of civilizations, with man, indestructible, holding his own. Hanya created a frontal, two-dimensional view of the dancing bodies rather than having the dancers seen in a circular view. This work contained some exciting scenes of early primitive and Aztec culture, and for the male dancers Hanya created an impressive dance of exorcism.

In the previous year, 1947, Hanya had experimented with words again, but this time she attacked a bigger problem than what she had done with *Namesake.* She joined forces with the drama department of the College and choreographed as well as directed *The Insect Comedy* by Karel and Josef Capek under the title *And So Ad Infinitum.* The play is a pessimistic allegory of man's rapaciousness and stupidity as seen through the insect world. In the first-act world of the butterflies we see the pettiness of love; in the second-act world the rivalries of families and existence as lived by beetles, crickets, and flies; in the third act, the tendency to war is illustrated by the ant world. Prologue and epilogue, populated by humans, emphasize the eternal life cycle.

The play was acted and danced by Hanya's dancers, and unaccompanied by music. The closest to music was the use of a metronome to indicate the passing of time when the ants entered the scene. The timing for the dancers' movement came from their own dynamics, the pulse of their breathing. "As visualized by the dramatists the insects were real people and acted as such," Hanya says. "The leading butterfly, for instance, acted as if she were a debutante; the beetles were Mr. and Mrs. Bourgeois and the ants, the workers, which entered from the orchestra pit and also took their exits there, were not dancers with masks, but dancers representing people, engineers, an inventor, or a signal officer. I turned my student dancers into actors — Glen Tetley and Jack Moore were among them. I was fascinated by the idea of blending acting and dancing. From the very beginning I considered it as an experiment to find out how far I could go in combining both media."

And So Ad Infinitum was such a success that it was restaged as *The Insect Comedy* at the New York City Center with José Ferrer, George Coulouris, and Alexander Scourby the very same season.

Hanya brought several of her creations from Colorado Springs to New York, but in those many summers from 1941 on she had occasion to repeat only one of her New York dances in Colorado. It was a piece of Americana, the *Ozark Suite,* originally shown at the Brooklyn Academy of Music with star dancers Bambi Linn and Ray Harrison. It was restaged at the Fine Arts Center Theatre in 1957 and also the following year with Hanya's students, among whom were Elizabeth Harris, Molly Lynn, and Don Redlich.

The critics and a great many dance connoisseurs expressed their surprise that Hanya's *Davey Crockett* in the *Ballet Ballads,* which came to Broadway in 1948, was indigenously American.

They all overlooked that American folk material was no novelty to Hanya, that she had often treated it before. Besides *Namesake*, the *Suite of Four Dances*, and the *Ozark Suite*, she choreographed a *Walt Whitman Suite*, *What So Proudly We Hail*, and a *Sousa March*. The latter, staged for six men, was a bit of a spoof of military training.

When Hanya did *Metropolitan Daily* in the late thirties, her uncanny sense of humor in dance form was established and recognized as one of her great assets. There are very few choreographers who have a knack for humor. But Hanya has proved over several decades on the concert stage as well as in the Broadway world of the musical that wit and humor are native with her. Often for the sake of a balanced program or to satisfy the need for a funny finale in the workshop productions in Colorado Springs she had — nolens volens — to contribute a humorous number. It has always worked. "The hardest nut to crack," Hanya declares, "has always been the fact that an originally funny idea can die in the hands of the person who must project it. Since it is never a matter only of *what* is being done but *how* something is done, the humor must come from the dancer himself. Humor cannot be delivered prefabricated to the dancer. Superimposed, it loses its subtle twists. Sometimes, however, I have been able to make non-humorous people appear humorous through unexpected manipulation of timing."

It is Hanya's opinion that you can project humor by split-second timing of whatever the movement signifies in relation to a deadly serious event. It may be serious, but the way in which it is done — overdone, underdone, or not done at all, with an absence of intensity or by overstressing the intensity — makes whatever it is appear funny. Knowing that logic does not always necessarily make sense, she sometimes uses nonsensical sequences or the non-sequitur, which then through their nonsensicality begin to make sense again. The greatest surprise effect lies in the involuntary event in which the accepted normal is heightened into its ridiculous counterpart. Humor lives on the incongruities and contradictions in life, on the contrast of ideas. Hanya believes that humor must make a comment on the perhaps all too logical, too serious, too premeditated in life.

The summer of 1965 rounded out a quarter of a century of Hanya's association with Colorado College, and that year the summer session turned into a "Hanya Holm Dance Festival." Everyone likes to be recognized for what he has accomplished. Hanya is no exception to this rule and, although she protested by saying, "But, children, I'll be back next year," she accepted being the center of admiration and adoration with resigned joy. She may sometimes feel embarrassed about the showing of too much affection and she also tries to sidestep anything coming close to sentimentality. But even she herself was a bit awed by the span of time that had elapsed and by the many things that had been done by her at the foot of Pike's Peak. Not for one minute, however, did she forget that what she was able to do in Colorado Springs was due to the fact that Colorado College had offered her the freedom of so many opportunities.

Above all, it was there that she could experiment free from the many frightening pressures of Broadway "biz." Perhaps she might never have turned to directing a straight play had it not been for her experiment with Capek's *The Insect Comedy*. And the same holds true for opera: she had her first opportunity in this field when she worked on Douglas Moore's *The Ballad of Baby Doe* in Central City. Hanya has discovered an atmosphere congenial to her temperament in Colorado, a kindred spirit that is, so to speak, in the air, a spirit which her dreams and desires project in this mountainous land with its sweeping spaces. Sometimes a landscape complements a human being and helps to show the way to greater fulfillment. Since Hanya has her headquarters in New York, the Mecca of the modern dance in America, Colorado Springs and the summer months spent there have been an escape from routine and the daily struggle, from being one of the many, even though she was one of the great ones. Hanya could easily have spent her summers in the East participating in one of the major dance festivals. But she has preferred her splendid isolation in Colorado, even at the risk that the majority of the modern dance enthusiasts do not get to see what her students produce and what she herself has been choreographing for them.

Student workshop productions, of course, depend on the student material, which changes with each year. But summer after summer the level has been much the same, since in Hanya's knowing hands weaknesses are turned into fortes. Her sense of what is good theater makes itself felt in the way she guides and influences her students, even though she may sometimes seem to stand aside and merely watch the progress of the rehearsals. But on occasion a decisive word from her can change a whole choreographic concept.

In 1965, however, no student workshop production was planned, everything was geared to fêting Hanya. During the first week of August on three consecutive evenings, the dance festival took place. Six of Hanya's former students who had meanwhile made names for themselves in the dance world came to Colorado Springs either alone, to appear in solos, or with their groups. They came to dance without any compensation, only to say Thank you to Hanya and to wish her many happy returns of her summer sessions.

The program opened with a solo by Valerie Bettis, . . . *And the Earth Shall Bear Again* . . . , to music for prepared piano by John Cage. It was followed by Nancy McKnight Hauser's *Lyric Suite* to a Respighi score, presented by her own company, the Dance Guild Theater of St. Paul. *Tangents* was Don Redlich's solo preceding Elizabeth Harris in her collage, *Before the Music Ends*. The second part of the program opened with Murray Louis' solo, *Transcendencies*, followed by two more solos, Don Redlich's *Earthling* and Valerie Bettis's well-known *Desperate Heart*, which was danced to the poem by John Malcolm Brinnin with a Bernardo Segall score. This section closed with Murray Louis' duet from *Junk Dances* in which Mr. Louis partnered

Phyllis Lamhut. The third part of the evening was given over
to Alwin Nikolais, who presented excerpts from Part I of
Sanctum, for which he did the choreography, sound score, and
design. Phyllis Lamhut and Murray Louis were the soloists.
Qualified summer students were permitted to audition for participation in *Sanctum*, which needed a group of sixteen dancers,
and three more students from the summer classes had featured
parts: Beverly Cook, Alma Martínez, and Wilson Barrileaux.
Klaus Holm honored his mother by designing the lighting and
supervising the technical aspects of the entire production.

There was a marked variety in this program of tribute to a
teacher, and it displayed the many facets of her students. There
was lyricism as smoothly visualized as in Bettis's opening number and in Hauser's suite; dramatic expressiveness in the *Desperate Heart*; the subtle shading of muscular virtuosity was
seen in both Don Redlich pieces; sophisticated wit with the help
of fantastic props and some terrifying aspects of modern life
were in the "way out" collage of Elizabeth Harris's *Before the
Music Ends*; poetic imagination and theatrical effectiveness were
combined in Murray Louis' *Transcendencies* and liberating
laughter in the lampooning of his *Junk Dances*; finally there
was the architectural moving of groups of depersonalized bodies aided by the movement of personalized props and by the
magic employment of light and sound in Nikolais' *Sanctum*.

Was it not all different from the Hanya Holm style? It was,
and yet the point of departure of all these different styles goes
back to the teaching genius of one teacher.

In other words, this program demonstrated, if nothing else,
that Hanya's approach to teaching is based on an intensive but
generally valid discipline imposing no definite style on the individual. Hanya strongly believes that when her method is
properly absorbed, the technical development can never lead to
a single style; on the contrary, it liberates the inner personality
and gives it the freedom of finding itself. She would often
tell her students, be it in New York or Colorado: "You have a
perfect right to branch out, *if* you have the stuff in you, *if* you

discover your own richness, *if* you have something to say."
Hanya has never cared what kind of technique a dancer employs. "What I want to see is a sign of passion. I want to see
the raw *it* struggling to express itself. A work must have
blood."

HANYA'S LYRIC THEATER

The Musical

MOST of us probably have a wrong notion of how dances are created for musicals. Who, for instance, would think that Frederic Loewe did not really write the music for the dances in *My Fair Lady*? That, with the songs ready, the music for the dances was done as an extension of the songs while Hanya was choreographing? "Their themes were used," Hanya explains, "but I had a composer for the dances with me all the time." This was Trude Rittman, whom Hanya had with her on most shows. The person who arranges the music for the dances usually receives a brief credit line in small print on the program bills. The fact that the dance music is arranged by a specially chosen composer who adapts the composer's melodies for the dances is hardly ever noticed by the audience.

But to begin at the beginning: after a thorough study of the script, the characters, and the music, many production meetings take place at which the choreographer can suggest placement of the dance routines. Once this decision is made, the real work begins. There are long hours of consultation with the set and costume designers. From these persons Hanya learns the exact amount of space she can have for her dances and the kind of clothing that is planned for the participants. Hanya says she always plans her dances with sketches of the costumes in front of her. In some cases — as in *My Fair Lady* — a compromise between the choreographer and the designer of set and costumes has to be worked out, and it is at this point that understanding and cooperation are most important.

The types of character portrayed naturally influence the style of dance designated for them. The entire action of all the characters is planned from the beginning of the scene to the end. None of the movements in dance numbers is accidental. Everything must be planned, according to Hanya. Occasionally parts of a dance may be developed during the usual four- or five-week rehearsal period, particularly to suit the abilities of certain featured dancers, and some of the planned steps may have to be altered since the choreographer works with the dancers' bodies as a sculptor works with clay. "The imagination in creating dances may be unlimited, but the execution of certain ideas is sometimes impossible," Hanya says, "since at all times the capabilities of the dancers must be considered."

The entire musical is polished during its trial run in cities outside New York or during previews in New York. Sometimes the polishing is extensive, in other cases everything has been right from the very beginning. Neither in *Kiss Me, Kate*, Hanya's first Broadway hit, nor in *My Fair Lady*, probably her crowning achievement, was a single dance routine changed.

It was a memorable Friday, this April 27 in 1948. The event itself, however joyful and successful, was not as important as were the tremendous consequences it brought: it wedded Hanya to the lyric theater, to the Broadway musical. And this in spite of the fact that the event took place in a small theater off Broadway, the Maxine Elliott Theatre. The occasion was the production of the *Ballet Ballads*. The libretto was written by the lyricist John Latouche, the score was by Jerome Moross. *Ballet Ballads*, produced by the Experimental Theatre, was an immediate success and, in due course, moved uptown to the Music Box Theatre.

On that decisive Friday Hanya received a call and was asked whether she would take over the chore of the choreography for "The Eccentricities of Davey Crockett," the third of the three ballet ballads. She would have only until Monday to prepare herself and then ten days rehearsal. "It was such a short notice that I had no time to think of how difficult it might be," Hanya says, "or even how scared I was to take over. I had the experience of *The Insect Comedy*, which gave me a basis of operation. I looked through the script and could accept libretto and music but not the stage direction, which were done from a purely literary point of view. I had to have something more three-dimensional. John Latouche had a different stage conception from what I thought Davey Crockett should look like, but he was very quickly convinced that the way I wanted to do it was the better way of doing it. I encountered no difficulties; on the contrary, I received the best cooperation imaginable from everyone concerned."

"The Eccentricities of Davey Crockett" was the last of three separate lyric pieces which formed the spiritual entity of *Ballet Ballads*, the other two being "Susanna and the Elders" (choreographed by Katherine Litz) and "Willie the Weeper" (choreographed by Paul Godkin). "The Eccentricities of Davey Crockett" consisted of a series of Davey's exploits as sung chiefly by himself: his adventures with a comet and with marauding Indians, the building of his house in the wilderness, his happy hooking of a mermaid, his courtship and marriage. This ballet ballad pictured Davey Crockett in terms of his own tall tales, with the chorus, the hero-worshipping Americans, assembled to celebrate the memory of his fantastic exploits. These were humorous visions of Davey's adventures, and, though there was a certain continuity in the telling of the story, there was neither a plot line nor a strong formal development to take its place.

Walter Terry referred to this weakness of the story line when he wrote in his Sunday piece: "Miss Holm has done a magnificent job of choreography, highlighting dance when action was required and subduing movement when it was right for song or acting to take the lead. 'Davey' may be loose dramatically, but thanks to Miss Holm its looseness of structure is transformed into disciplined agility." John Martin commented that "its great good fortune is that Hanya Holm is its choreographer, for she has supplied it with witty and imaginative movement throughout. One quite delightful dance about a bear hunt by six men is the best moment of the evening. In addition to all this, she alone of the three choreographers has managed to mix the singers with the dancers without making them look as if all their feet were left ones."

Almost everyone was struck by the unpretentious folk quality of the Davey Crockett piece, by its freshness, excitement, and Americanism. Hanya surprised with her uncanny intuitive feeling, with which she was able to re-create a characteristically American legend with the right indigenous shares in color and style. But — we must not forget — she had treated American material previously for the concert stage and proved that this was far from alien to her. Moreover, the character of Davey Crockett — however American his background might be — had a close European relative.

"It was a story very similar to our own story of Baron Münchhausen," Hanya says, "which is sheer eccentric fantasy, but of course a fantasy which grew on Central European soil. Both heroes took the impossible for granted, both stretched the imagination to the point of 'nuttiness.' The reviewers stressed the point that I caught the spirit of Davey Crockett so well. The truth is that I knew very little about him before I started to work on the show. I had to familiarize myself with the legend practically overnight. But it wasn't difficult. His adventures made my own fantasy work, and I never think in terms of translating something literally. When I came to this country my very first exercises were to find out what makes America the America it is. As an outsider I had an objective point of view, and my impression was not superficial, not just like a movie reeling off, but it was an impression nourished by experience. So I could give my fantasy free reign without any outside interference.

"We had a basic set consisting of three bleachers built of solid iron. Steps led into the iron construction so that the dancers could be easily moved. All three bleachers were identical, but two of them where the steps were visible formed a horseshoe, the center piece turned to the steps that led upstage and served as entrance to the platform on top of the bleachers, a platform that gave us enough space to move around. And center upstage there was another entrance coming from underneath the steps which I used to great advantage in the bear hunt. I could also easily stage the mermaid scene, with the mermaid coming out of the water and slipping behind Davey. Then we built a house in the center of the stage during the Indian scene. Shortly, everything was used in absolutely organic fashion with no real changes whatsoever, but the miraculous thing was that the set, rigid as it seemed, changed with the mood in relationship to the action that took place."

Within a few months after this success Hanya was acclaimed with even more resonant intensity. Things happened to her, and Hanya followed them willingly. "I have not been a part of the legitimate theater in America," she says. "Neither at this nor at any other point have I made up my mind or decided on working in the theater. True, I have been devoted to the theater all my life, but at that time it was the theater of the concert field. Again, I came to *Kiss Me, Kate* without any preparatory work, also without any questions of doubt. This was my first big Broadway assignment — can I or can't I do it? Should I accept or should I not? Apparently the offer was made based on what I had done before in the theatrical field, *Trend, Insect Comedy*, and "Davey Crockett." They all were different but theatrically challenging and taxing tasks. People seemed to have found out that there was an open mind which could adjust itself to all kinds of theatrical ventures. So they asked me whether I would be interested in choreographing *Kiss Me, Kate*. I said I would have to have some more information on what had to be done. I warned them that I could not be different from what I am but that I would try and do my job to the best of my abilities. I had to go through a third-degree interrogation, but apparently to everyone's satisfaction. So I started to work on it. That it turned out to be so successful no one could have known in the beginning."

Nor could Hanya know that this cleverly written story of a

vainglorious actor and his temperamental ex-wife, who are starring in a revival of *The Taming of the Shrew* in Baltimore, would turn out to be such a dancy show. The rehearsals were a period of unexpected demands. Problems popped up in every scene, necessities arose as she worked along, necessities for which solutions had to be found on the spur of the moment. It was different from whatever Hanya had done before, and the situations had to be mastered. It was usually a question of finding an imaginative extension of what was sung. "For instance, in the song of the 'Special Face,'" Hanya explains, "there was something left unfulfilled, it needed an imaginative idea, so I invented the Dark Lady who appeared in black with a fan in the *commedia dell'arte* fashion, and I gave her very quick movements."

Kiss Me, Kate had a clever book by Bella and Samuel Spewack as well as scintillating lyrics and music by Cole Porter. *Variety* recognized immediately at the show's tryout in Philadelphia that it had all the ingredients of a hit show and also mentioned that "Hanya Holm has done a neat job by the choreography." When *Kiss Me, Kate* opened at the New Century Theatre on December 30, 1948, it was unanimously greeted as another milestone in the development of the American musical.

The many critical kudos pointed out that Hanya's dances were individually profiled and effervescent, demanding great skill without ever suggesting a muscle-flexing contest. They had the rare gift of making each dancer look as if he had a purpose in what he was doing. And this is exactly what Hanya has always aimed for.

There was no great ballet number as such in the show, but there was dancing almost everywhere, all of it firmly integrated with the purpose of achieving a total theatrical impression. The dancing became impetus and driving element in this musical and provided the means for transitions in pace, mood, and style. The range of the dance forms used was impressive. It embraced classic ballet, modern dance, jitterbugging, soft-shoe, acro-

batics, court, and folk dance. And there were many minor episodes characteristic of rhythmic playfulness. John Martin, in
one of his Sunday columns, best summed up Hanya's accomplishment:

> Nobody could have stepped more gracefully into a new field
> than Hanya Holm has done in her transition from the concert
> dance to show business. The dances she has created for *Kiss Me,
> Kate* are her first for a Broadway musical, but they have about
> them the ease and finish of a veteran. What is equally note-
> worthy, they have retained the taste, the formal integrity and the
> respect for the movement of the human body which belong to
> the concert dance, without in the least disturbing the equanimity
> of the paying customers.
> The surface of Miss Holm's dances, ranging as it does fre-
> quently into the hot and the blue and the jittery, is so remote
> from what she has done in the past that there is a temptation to
> be startled, even to feel a momentary doubt that she could have
> had anything to do with it. But one who knows his Holm soon
> realizes that, paradoxically enough, the very atypicalness of it
> all makes it typical. . . .
> The choreography is at all times completely of the texture of
> the show. Nowhere from the rise of the first curtain to the fall
> of the last, is there a characteristic Holm movement; she has ap-
> parently not been tempted in the least to superimpose herself
> upon the production but has given her attention wholly to bring-
> ing out and pointing up what is inherent in it.

By then Hanya was very much aware of her working methods: "If I keep my mind open, my imagination seems to be one
step ahead. Sometimes thought and action occur simultaneously. I may do something that is wrong, but when I look at it
with a critical eye I realize immediately whether I was right or
wrong. But I have to keep up the same spirit, otherwise I wreck
it. I must fix it at once, otherwise I might start constructing and
I am wary of too much cerebralness. Fortunately, most of the
time there is immediately an intuitive veto, a feeling that holds
me back if something goes wrong."

A history-making event in the dance field accompanied
the success of *Kiss Me, Kate*. Hanya, who had always strongly

believed in Labanotation, asked Ann Hutchinson to notate the dances during the rehearsals of *Kiss Me, Kate*. The notation was finished sometime after the opening night, and in March 1952 Hanya registered the first complete choreographic score of the dances for copyright in Washington. The entire script, photographed on microfilm, is now on file at the Library of Congress.

Hanya's action has served several important purposes. It has given a certain official approval to dance notation and put it on a similar level with music notation. It has given the choreographer the possibility to be recognized as the owner of his own work, and it has established a choreographic composition as an entity apart from any specific performance of it. Three important elements have thus been served: technological progress, property rights, and the tangibility of artistic creation in the dance field.

The use of Labanotation was — at least to some degree — put to the test when, in 1951, *Kiss Me, Kate* was produced in the Coliseum in London. The dances could be rehearsed on the basis of the notation, but in this particular case, because of the enormous size of the Coliseum's stage, Hanya had to adjust the choreography to its new environment and help the conductor become familiar with the movements. But under ordinary circumstances notation has proved its value time and again, and Hanya has often made use of it.

In 1950 Hanya became involved in the choreography of *The Liar*. "For me there is nothing that does not offer some satisfaction," Hanya says. "Also *The Liar* had its merits although it did not work out at all. I simply look at it as another chance to deal with another problem and other limitations. Particularly the set created handicaps which we had to overcome and we did it as best was possible. In general, this set provided limited space for the dancers and left little for the imagination to work on."

The Liar is based on one of the many Carlo Goldoni plays. The story takes place in the sixteenth century and concerns a day in the mendacious life of a young Venetian whose total disregard for speaking the truth leads him into all kinds of mischief and ridiculous complications. Goldoni, who emulated Molière but in none of his works came close to his greatness, had written the play in the early eighteenth-century manner, with innumerable asides which the musical did not eliminate. If nothing else, the many asides and an unwieldly set were severe difficulties in giving the show the lightness of the *commedia dell'arte atmosphere* which it needed.

Norris Houghton began to direct the show, but very soon gave up, and Alfred Drake, who wrote the libretto together with Edward Eager, took over the direction. At that time Mr. Drake was still playing the lead in *Kiss Me, Kate* and traveling back and forth to Philadelphia, where *The Liar* had its tryout. *The Liar* was one of Alfred Drake's pet ideas, and he had gone through gruelling auditions for several years to find financial backing for the show.

John Mundy had written a few nice tunes for *The Liar*, but the show was turned down by the reviewers and the public alike. On April 24, 1950, the musical opened its tryout at the Forrest Theater in Philadelphia. The immediate reaction was one of severe disappointment. It was obvious that the cast was not up to its task and the direction was in many ways faulty, indecisive, and unconvincing. Such a complicated but obvious plot with its popular stamp of the eighteenth century should have been treated with lightning wit, perhaps in a rather quaint but certainly in a more colorful manner.

When the show came to the Broadhurst Theatre on May 18, 1950, Robert Coleman expressed the reaction of many when he wrote in the *Daily Mirror:* "It is not a pleasant task this morning to report that *The Liar* . . . is a pedestrian and dull musical."

Other difficulties to the detriment of theatrical fulfillment also beset the next show with which Hanya was connected, *Out of This World.* The main trouble was that it was another Amphytrion story, "Amphytrion 39" if we accept Giraudoux's counting. Hanya was aware that a great many things ought to have been done theatrically to offset the uneven libretto. But the most obvious devices could not be employed because they had been used before. Many of these ideas were copyrighted, and the cry of plagiarism would have been loud. Thus, Hanya admits, many things were done out of necessity and not because they were the best and most colorful notions.

In Philadelphia, where the tryout began, the feeling was that this Cole Porter show offered a rich fare but that there was something distinctly wrong with it. In Boston the apprehensive feeling remained the same, but there at least one was certain that the show was too sexy. "Clean it up or get it out of town," the papers said. Janet Collins in her dance as Night had to put on more clothes.

Originally the direction was in the hands of Agnes de Mille, but George Abbott, the troubleshooter, was called in to doctor the show. "This work was difficult," Hanya says, "because it was not downright show dancing, but rather lyric theater that had its 'showy' moments. It made the theater an integrated thing rather than a showplace for separate people and numbers." But though the show may have approached a total theater production, it was unable to overcome the handicaps basic with the book, which was written by Dwight Taylor and Reginald Lawrence. The free flow of imagination was curtailed in this case by the well-known story; moreover, casting troubles added to the travails.

When *Out of This World* arrived at the Century Theatre in New York its reception was mixed. Brooks Atkinson maintained that "although it is difficult to make sex a tiresome subject, *Out of This World* has nearly succeeded." William Hawkins remarked in the *New York World Telegram:* "The male dancing chorus is almost as unhampered by godlike raiment as the costumes in a steam bath. Hanya Holm has directed them to create a kind of pagan innocence which is not usually characteristic of the show's humor."

The dancing in any musical is inherently dependent on the

framework of the story, music, set, and costumes; in other words, on pretty much everything that lies outside its own creative impulse. The dances are usually doomed if the show is doomed to fail. But in the case of *Out of This World* Hanya proved a strong, independent spirit, and her choreographic skill triumphed in spite of, or apart from, the irremediable difficulties of the show.

John Martin analyzed the dances apart from the meritorious or meretricious value of the show in *The New York Times:*

> She has given us, indeed, just about as stunning a set of dances as a Broadway show has boasted in a couple of seasons.
>
> As admirers of *Kiss Me, Kate* will recall, her numbers there were . . . unpretentious in the extreme, never stepping outside the structure of the scene, never begging for applause, but invariably contributing charm and value by heightening the motor rhythms of the situation and building them easily and ingratiatingly to a climax. She has employed the same approach in *Out of This World,* but possibly because the subject-matter is more grateful choreographically, she has been even more effective with it.
>
> She is no prima donna choreographer who builds up her own numbers and then tries to drape the rest of the show around them; what she does grows simply and logically out of the situation, the characters, the atmosphere of the piece, and as a consequence, they are rich in style and individuality. They are also rich in invention and in formal design. The paying customers are not aware that they care about such things but they do. Miss Holm's dances in *Out of This World* are definitely a hit, and one of the chief reasons is that though she is a high brow and a longhair and all the rest of it, right out of the modern dance concert field, she does not look down her nose at the Broadway medium. Recognizing its texture and its dimensions, she treats them with the imagination and respect which any creative form demands.
> . . .
> Jupiter has descended from Olympus to encompass a mortal maiden. Miss Holm has set the air shimmering. Half a dozen couples move in amorous eagerness, each of them different from all the rest, while the grinning figure of Pan stands with bent knees on a tree stump, holding them together with his eye, or joins them momentarily for a twirl or a violent thrust of the hip.

There are bold leaps and lifts, attitudes of taut suspense. Now at one side of the scene stands a figure with hands vibrating over his head; on the other side the vibration is echoed in a torso, a thigh. It is a truly magic evocation, a lyric poem of the deepest dignity for all its frank voluptuousness.

The year was 1956. The musical was *My Fair Lady*, based on George Bernard Shaw's *Pygmalion*. Book and music were by Alan Jay Lerner and Frederic Loewe, who had proved their mettle in *Brigadoon*. Cecil Beaton designed the sets and costumes. Moss Hart directed. Julie Andrews, Rex Harrison, and Stanley Holloway were the stars. It was the biggest hit Broadway had seen since *Oklahoma!*, and it turned out to be even bigger. It had its national road companies, was duplicated in London and produced in almost all big cities of the world. Then came the film version which has been seen everywhere. The people shouted "Wow!" and the critics echoed their surprise and joy. For them it was just a matter of finding the right superlative, the most glowing and colorful adjective. Even if that adjective was cliché-ridden and corny, it no longer mattered. This was it!

Hanya staged the musical numbers, which included a Tottenham Court Road number for Doolittle's song, "With a Little Bit of Luck"; a pseudo-Spanish extravaganza for Eliza's triumphant elocution number, "The Rain in Spain Stays Mainly in the Plain"; an "Ascot Gavotte" for the race-meeting scene which took the place of the celebrated tea party; and the waltz in the ballroom of the Embassy. There was in between some incidental stage movement here and there for which Hanya must be credited, but the biggest pure dance number was set in Covent Garden Market early in the morning, when flower girls and market porters join in a jubilant Cockney number with the refrain "Get Me to the Church on Time."

Mainly on account of this number, but also to absorb the entire London atmosphere in which *Pygmalion* was born and without which it could not have come alive, Hanya, the perfectionist, went to London. She made a special point of getting up early, or rather of staying up late, in order to be among the people in Covent Garden Market at its busiest time with the break of dawn.

"Well, there was a situation full of realities," Hanya notes. "It was a must for me to have been there, to have seen it. Of course, it is a question of empathy, of genuine *Einfühlung*, in order to create a proper stage realization of reality. Because, in the theater, you cannot translate anything verbatim. I was fortunate enough to have seen the last few buskers in London, the street entertainers who try to make a few pennies performing for people who have to queue up for buses. These entertainers also would suddenly stop at a street corner to perform. I once saw a few of them with a drum and some hidden paraphernalia. I followed and observed how they performed at several corners. The pants were quickly curled up, something funny-looking was thrown around the neck, a ridiculous-looking hat was put on, a Charlie Chaplin cane became visible all of a sudden. In no time a little circle of people formed around them. The minute a policeman was in sight they disappeared, only to perform at another corner. Their movements were mainly acrobatic, and they did all sorts of stances in order to entertain. I used the buskers in Scene One, but absorbing the London street scene in general stimulated me quite a bit.

"I had great fun doing the Flower Market scene," Hanya reminisces. "I also could use all the time I wanted for this dance. Because of the unlimited possibilities at my disposal, this dance number was complete in itself, the way it began and faded out. The Ascot Gavotte also was a number that emerged from the very beginning as something right and inevitable. I hit the bull's eye with the first few steps. Everything came very natural to me, I did not have to throw out any material, I only shaved it a bit here and there, as in the process of creating one usually winds up with more material than one actually needs. Since horse races in Europe were often combined with fashion shows, it was obvious to create the dance as a little fashion show; in other words, it became a composition with a means to an end. It had to be properly stylized, otherwise it would not have worked. I had the benefit of those wonderful costumes which were adjusted to the need of the choreography. This shows how it feels to work with people who are sure of themselves and, therefore, can afford to cooperate. Trouble only starts if you face coworkers who do not know what they want or who are limited to one idea and then think that this is it. These people cannot accept that someone else may have another problem whose solution may depend on his cooperation. If cooperation is not achieved, if, for instance, the ego of a costume or scene designer is overpowering, then only one thing suffers, and that is the show."

It seems that this artistic welding process is a secret, and it is what Gustave Flaubert must have meant when he said that the theater is not an art but a secret. It is probably the secret of creating something beyond the actual contribution, aiming at the ultimate, at a sum total in which no part is more important than the whole. In other words, the art of welding such a show to a point of perfection lies in the fact that every detail must be as important in itself as its relationship to the whole. Such a show must have a common denominator which reigns supreme. And if it then does not reach perfection, it may at least come close to the concept of total theater.

"Well, what makes a show a show?" Hanya asks. "It is very difficult to say, it is a mystery. What makes a human being a being? Why isn't a robot ever a human being? Because it has no inner life, no soul, it is just mechanics. Now something mechanical may excel in one aspect, but it cannot contribute to an integrated whole, to a perfect or near-perfect show."

Sometimes "contributing" may mean helping one's coworkers see the light or deleting something in a self-effacing manner. At one point Hanya decided to cut out an entire dance in My Fair Lady. It was in the scene in which Eliza got ready for the ball which would be her moment of truth. By then she had been thoroughly groomed, she had had all kinds of lessons, including her famous elocution lessons with marbles in her mouth. At this point of the musical the first version had Eliza sing "Say a Prayer for Me Tonight," accompanied by a montage of little events taking place simultaneously in an atmosphere of complete unreality, using everyone who contributed to her readiness for the ball, from the hairdresser to the costume-maker to the masseuse. This scene had great charm and humor, but it was obviously redundant with so many lessons and preparations preceding it. Alan Lerner was heartbroken when he felt forced to cut it and to find another transition. But Hanya insisted that the whole scene must be discarded and that a simpler and smoother transition must be found. Between the tryouts in New Haven and Philadelphia the scene was rewritten, and the most simplified approach to it worked best. "What Alan Lerner came up with was just the right solution," Hanya says. "He came up with the idea of the port wine scene. It worked beautifully. Anything else would have been wrong. You have to do these things sometimes. Even if it is a good dance it has to go, even if it is a wonderful song like "Say a Prayer for Me Tonight" — which I think landed later in *Gigi*. But even if it has to go for good it is not really wasted, it is a part of the creative process."

In New Haven, where the tryout started at the Shubert Theatre on February 4, 1956, it was immediately obvious that this was "a whale of a show," as *Variety* called it. The *New Haven Journal-Courier* termed the show "sensational in every respect," a phrase which telescopes the many affirmative and joyful descriptions into the simplest image of boundless enthusiasm. The newspapers in Philadelphia echoed the exuberant reactions of their New Haven counterparts, and when the show opened on Broadway Walter Kerr gave vent to the most natural impulse when he began his review in the *New York Herald Tribune* with the words: "Don't bother to finish reading this review now. You'd better sit right down and send for those tickets to *My Fair Lady*. First things first."

Hanya's dances were lauded along with everyone else's accomplishments. There were, of course, certain shades of preference in the general praise. Wolcott Gibbs of *The New Yorker* was hardly ever given to lyric exultations, but he referred to Hanya as having "staged at least two dances that struck me as being as lovely as dreams." Most sober was Brooks Atkinson's observation of Hanya's unique contribution, that she "has blended the dance numbers into the story so unobtrusively that they seem like extensions of the general theme in terms of motion."

John Martin contrasted the essence of dance with the didactic aims of George Bernard Shaw, who had said about the success of his play *Pygmalion*, "It is so intensely and deliberately didactic, and its subject so dry, that I delight in throwing it at the heads of the wiseacres who repeat the parrot cry that art should never be didactic. It goes to prove my contention that art should never be anything else." The musical version in no way challenged Shaw's contention or changed his basic intent, and this is one of the reasons for its having repeated — and even tripled — the success of the original play. The light-footed Terpsichore, particularly in show business, is never associated with didactic profundity and enlightenment. In this respect John Martin's remarks gain weight:

> The "Rain in Spain" song inevitably leads into suitable dance phrases, and when one adds up what occurs from curtain to curtain there is an enormous amount of dancing in the evening. Since dancing is the fullest basic medium of the lyric theatre, it stands to reason that it is also the most potent antidote to the Shavian podium. That they enrich each other instead of cancelling each other out is why Miss Holm . . . should be decorated.

Long before the birth of *My Fair Lady* Shaw was approached for permission to turn his *Pygmalion* into a musical. Infuriated, he snapped back at the solicitor in a characteristic Shavian attitude: "If *Pygmalion* is not good enough for your friends with its own verbal music, their talent must be altogether extraordinary." In *My Fair Lady*'s case, it was.

Its success did not stop on Broadway. Londoners queued up for tickets at Drury Lane Theatre seven months before the appointed first night. Everyone referred to its premiere as the biggest first night in the history of London's West End. Nor did its success stop in London. The Russians loved it, and so did the Australians. There was not a single city in Europe priding itself on its theater that did not see a production of this show. It ran on Broadway over six and a half years, and was revived at the City Center on May 20, 1964. Hanya flew to Israel, where she restaged the work at the Habimah National Theater in February of 1964.

Although there was only one big dance number with a great deal of incidental dancing, Hanya's imprint was felt to permeate the entire show. We know she can choreograph a rousing dance and fill the stage with joyful and enjoyable action. But one could feel her hand in every effective entrance, in the grace with which the actors danced, or rather acted as if they danced. It was the over-all pattern of motion which ran through the entire show, the bits and intimations of dances with which it was permeated and which created a feeling of fluidity and an inimitable entity of idea. *My Fair Lady* was a shining example of how the dance, even without the stunning staging of ballets or dance numbers, can cement a show and add a colorful glazing to its finish.

Hanya is so sure of herself and of what she has to contribute in order to make a scene come alive, to heighten a situation, to carry the action forward through motor rhythm, that she never feels compelled to step beyond the frame of the story to beg for applause.

An enjoyable trip to England was occasioned by Hanya's restaging of the old and proven warhorse *Where's Charley?* This Frank Loesser romp opened at the Opera House in Manchester on November 4, 1957. Norman Wisdom played the leading part and brought the house down. The *News Chronicle* and *Daily Dispatch* said that "the production by William Chappell is first-class, also the dances for which Hanya Holm . . . came from America to direct." And the *Manchester Evening*

News found that "there is effective choreography by Hanya Holm."

The show tells the simple-minded old tale of the Oxford student who dresses up as his aunt from Brazil in order to chaperone a naughty lunch party of the nineties. The *Daily Express* reported on February 21, 1958: "New to this English version — they did not have this in New York — was a breathtaking ballet devised by Hanya Holm. The appropriate theme, Brazil (where the nuts come from)."

"I loved it," Hanya says, "it was nice to do. The composer Frank Loesser allowed me to do the Pernambuco Ballet the way I wanted it because he wrote some music for it with which I could not do anything, so I did my own percussion. Thus, we had quite an interesting and exciting South American ballet in it. The entire production was like an original, it was quite fascinating to work with Norman Wisdom, who played himself. I had to concentrate on the type he represented to be able to use him to good advantage. This was another Charley from what we were used to see — which did not change the show, but gave it another character. It was an indigenous English Charley with wonderful nuances which would not have been understood in New York. The whole thing had a lot of style and something of its own. Every point was understood. I enjoyed doing it very much."

Two years later came the musical *Christine*, of which Hanya says, "Despite its failure I got a lot out of it. We had excellent dances but dance alone cannot save a show." Walter Kerr worded it differently when he saw the show at the 46th Street Theatre on April 28, 1960: "Every 15 minutes or so choreographer Hanya Holm gathers together her truly skilled troupe, including a few obviously genuine Indians who know how to behave like cobras, for a swift rattle of ankle-bells and a roar of percussion in the pit. Miss Holm's work seemed to me to be excellent, and generally uncalled for."

Pearl S. Buck's book had the features of a travelogue, pointing out many of the quaint customs of Indian civilization and dwelling on the prejudices and ignorance of the natives. Its story line concerned an American mother (played by Maureen O'Hara) who went to India to visit her daughter and unwanted son-in-law, an Indian physician. The mother finds her daughter has died in childbirth. The Indian physician and the mother-in-law fall in love.

It was a beautifully mounted musical with colorful costumes and lovely sets, which were praised. But it was dull and trite. Neither the music by Sammy Fain nor Hanya's entrancing dances could save the show. "Bhaskar did both a cobra appeasement dance and a village festival dance," Hanya remembers. "He was my assistant and advised me to keep the spirit of the dancing Eastern. Even if the Eastern dances somewhat departed from Eastern style, its idiom was still there. On the other hand, the American dancers had to learn the Eastern style. Bhaskar gave all dancing the atmosphere of authenticity."

Kenneth Tynan said in *The New Yorker:* "Hanya Holm's choreography brightens the prevailing gloom with a series of routines in which Burmese, Irish, Georgian, Cossack, Indian, American Indian, and Minsky styles are inventively blended."

Although the same people worked on *Camelot* as on *My Fair Lady,* that did not assure that *Camelot* would become another *My Fair Lady.* It did not. It was based on T. H. White's *The Once and Future King,* and White wrote about a man who is far ahead of his time. That man is Arthur, and the novel describes his evolution as an apostle of peace and reason. He is put to the test when an innocent love affair between his wife Guinevere and Lancelot, his noblest, bravest, and dearest friend, endangers the stability of his kingdom. With this event, prejudice and suspicion get the upperhand. The ideals of the Round Table are contemptuously repudiated; civil war breaks out. In the end Lancelot has fled, Guinevere is in a nunnery, and Arthur's hopes lie in ruins. But even though the reality seems to negate it, his ideal of peace and order persists.

Speaking of the days when they worked on the show, Hanya says: "It had its trials and tribulations aplenty. There were many side events and little stories added to the main story line. The show lasted four hours when we arrived with it in Toronto, where it was tried out first. We had our troubles with sickness, and yet the cutting had to be done. Cutting in shows is a major operation. It's like surgery. You not only cut something out, you must also put something in to hold it together. What you add on as new material matters a great deal because there has to be a balance in each show, it has to be restored or created where it is missing. This is so important because a whole scene may have to be written in as a connecting link. Sometimes a whole dance has to go out or others have to come in. I was fortunate in not losing any dances during the severe reshaping of the show because at the very beginning I had suggested dances only where I thought they were necessary to further the show. In principle I am against a dance substituting for the lack of an idea. The dances must be a part of the action, the extension of a symbol — a necessity, not a substitute. It is so easy for the writer of a libretto to suggest a dance at a certain spot when he does not know what else to do. But then the dance stands out like a sore thumb, there is an awkward feeling to it when it comes at that very point of the show.

"In my estimation it was a worthwhile show, one with a timely message and great meaning for our age. The message was clearly spelled out by the idea of the Round Table, the uniting of nations, the exclusion of wars, the attempt at settling differences in an atmosphere of mutual understanding and in a civilized manner. That really interested me and attracted me to Camelot. From a theatrical viewpoint the love story was of course of prime importance. Though it was not as perfect a show as My Fair Lady, I enjoyed working with the same people. I had full cooperation from everyone. Richard Burton, who played the lead, enjoyed doing his little dance, he was all eagerness and willingness. I remember when there was a half-hour layover for him in Boston during the performances, he practiced the dance. He always wanted to do it again and again. It did not come to him the easy way as the tango came to Rex Harrison in *My Fair Lady*. Yes, sometimes all that is needed is time."

Hanya was invited to do the choreography for *Tannhäuser* at the Metropolitan Opera House for that season. But because of the extended repair work on *Camelot* and the delays encountered in the final production of the musical, she was forced to withdraw from this assignment.

The first tryouts of *Camelot* were at the O'Keefe Centre in Toronto. It opened there on October 1, 1960. The general consensus was that this show offered an embarrassment of riches without shape, that it was charming but asked for a great deal of work to be done on it. Boston, where *Camelot* started at the Shubert Theatre on October 28, found that its visual aspects were gorgeous but the book dull, that it had all the ingredients of a long-run and distinguished hit except a lively libretto. There was objection, too, to its message of peace and justice, because this didactic quality seemed fatal to some believers in sheer entertainment.

When *Camelot* opened at the Majestic Theatre on December 3, it had changed somewhat, but it was not able to shake off the basic flaws with which it was born. The general reaction was one of mixed feelings and puzzlement. It was obviously a very handsome musical play with many lovely and imaginative episodes. But heavy clouds were hanging over it, the going was slow and confused. From time to time the show got lost amid its fantasy, its satirical humor, and its romantic wistfulness.

Where the show really shone was in the brilliance of its pageantry in such scenes as the opening processional, the gay May party, the grandstand of the jousting field, the conferring of knighthood in the Great Hall. During the summer following the opening of *Camelot*, Hanya said in an interview in Colorado Springs: "Dances are peppered all through the show. There's a dance in an enchanted forest, a riot of fantasy; and a May-Day dance, largely folk idiom, and loads of other dances, processions, jousts, and fun-makers. I don't have to be puny so long as I stay within bounds and so long as the dances develop the scene, widen it out, give it bigger scope. My ideas come from the demands of the whole content of the show, where a dance not only must climax a scene, but must lead back into what must follow."

In 1964 and 1965 there were successful revivals of *My Fair Lady* and *Kiss Me, Kate* at the New York City Center, and in the fall of 1965 Hanya was involved in choreographing and staging the musical numbers for a new musical, called *Anya*. It was based on the story of Anastasia, who claimed to be the daughter of the last Russian Czar and the only member of the family to survive the revolution. Tunes of Rachmaninoff were shaped to fit this musical, which could not liberate itself from the mannerisms of the old operetta. *Anya* was another example of how a faulty book can doom a show.

When it opened at the Ziegfeld Theatre on November 29, 1956, Martin Gottfried, critic of *Women's Wear Daily*, condemned the musical but added: "The final big contributor was Hanya Holm, who created too little choreography, all of which was charming and very well danced." Public and press alike rejected *Anya* as an old-fashioned, sentimental musical that lacked distinction and lightness.

"Many lovely dances had to be left out," Hanya says; "it was a very uneven show. The music had to be used as it was, therefore we had to adjust to it. Whole sections were taken out, and the dancers were left without enough music to dance to. A dancer doesn't live on one, two, three jump! He has to work up a certain excitement, he has to get into whatever he wants to do, and if that is cut out, then there is little left for him. One can't have only climaxes without seeing how one gets to them. For me, the dance is an essential element in the lyric theater. It can give it bounce and character. I don't like to fool around with it and I loathe situations in which I do not have full cooperation and a free creative hand. Show business is, as far as I am concerned, a serious business."

To listen to music is not enough, you must have it in the body.

— Hanya Holm

The Opera

Hanya's staging of the operas *The Ballad of Baby Doe* and *Orpheus and Eurydice* was a joyful experience. The former took place in Central City, Colorado; the Gluck opera was premiered in Vancouver and then repeated in Toronto. But before she had the opportunity to be involved in the presentation of these two works, she had done preparatory work in the operatic medium.

It may be argued that *My Darlin' Aida, Reuben, Reuben,* and *The Golden Apple,* the three productions which preceded Hanya's excursion into the operatic field, were musicals. From the viewpoint of their presentation and advance publicity they may have been musicals, but generically they must be considered as operatic endeavors since the problems they posed to the choreographer were those of operas. All three librettos were set to music throughout, instead of having songs inserted among spoken lines.

My Darlin' Aida (produced at the Winter Garden in October 1952) was Verdi's opera with not a single note changed and only the music for one dance section added. Charles Friedman had the idea of translating the libretto into terms of the American South during the Civil War years. Aida, a plantation slave, loves Captain Raymond Demarest (Radames in the original), who is unhappily pledged to Jessica Farrow (Amneris), daughter of the plantation owner (Pharaoh). Aida's stepfather, Adam Brown (Amonasro), returns from the North via the underground to lead an uprising of the slaves, and the Captain becomes involved in the rebellion. The plot, however, is discovered, Brown is shot, Aida is wounded, and Captain Demarest is fatally whipped by a gathering of masked and hooded Knights of the White Cross. The lovers die together in a rickety old Negro church while outside in the graveyard Jessica prays for the repose of Demarest's soul.

In adjusting Verdi's opera and the choreography to its new environment, the challenge rested with the imposed limitations. "Rarely has a choreographer sacrificed herself so deliberately as choreographer to the good of the production as a whole." This was the way John Martin opened his review, which recognized the many problems Hanya faced. The dance of the priestesses had to be cut altogether. The dance of the Moorish boys in Amneris' chamber had to be turned into the excited cavorting of three maidens dressing a Southern belle for a festival. The translation of the triumphal scene into terms of the American Civil War posed the greatest difficulties. It "has been handled with wonderful dexterity, though it has lost most of its dance values in the process," Mr. Martin wrote. There was a brief military drill, a carnival show with a magician, Moorish clowns and hootch dancers.

Where Hanya came into her own was in a scene in the second act. It took place in the slave quarters, where a group of Negroes moved into a lively dance under high dramatic motivation. "There we had to make the music for ourselves," Hanya says, "since it was not provided in the score. And we made it by rattling of bones, pounding on barrelheads, we used drums, tin cans, sticks, and scraped on a washboard. Anything was used that could be found on plantation grounds and that made noise. Of course, I had the dancers whistle and hum. That was the only point where we deviated from the original score." This dance was stunning and exciting; it had formal integrity and managed to capture the emotional exuberance of the plantation Negroes.

"It was a very beautiful and rewarding production, financially not successful as it was too expensive. Scene designer Lemuel Ayers did a wonderful job. The set had the Southern opulence and lush beauty, one could never forget the Spanish moss hanging down. It was in great style and had a spectacular quality, it had color and, of course, the unbeatable music by Verdi," Hanya says.

Two years later John Latouche and Jerome Moross came up with the daring idea of using the story of the Iliad and the Odyssey in an American locale around the turn of the century. The result was called *The Golden Apple,* and its story unfolded in the State of Washington, the apple country. Homer's well-known figures are all there: Ulysses and Penelope, Hector and Achilles, Calypso and Circe. Paris, a traveling salesman, lures Helen, a bucolic strumpet, off to the city. Ulysses, a muscular-brained Spanish-American war hero, leaves his peaceful home and Penelope to bring Helen back. In the process of this courageous enterprise he gets rid of Paris, dallies with Circe and her siren sisters, and gets involved with Hector, whose last name is Charybdis and who is partner in a crooked stock-market operation to a man named Scylla.

There was no spoken line to interrupt the music. But *The Golden Apple* was not so much an opera as almost a new genre which could be termed a dance opera. Hanya's recollections of this wonderful adventure of *The Golden Apple* indicate that "the whole thing was danced from the beginning to the end, it was inevitable to visualize and plan each phase from a choreographic point of view. Every scene had another problem, with the two Homer stories being interwoven and juxtaposed and the Helen of Troy story always kept in the foreground of interest."

The Golden Apple demanded a highly inventive staging because of its inherently literary concept, which superimposed an American setting upon a mythological legend. The staging was eminently successful because it avoided the pitfalls of telling the story in realistic terms. Every scene needed the imaginative extension of movement. "There is almost nothing in *The Golden Apple* that looks like a dance 'routine,' yet Miss Holm's mark is strong upon the whole production," John Martin wrote. "The direction is not credited to her but it has manifestly felt her shaping influence.... Her idea is ... to make the production not a 'book' with choreographic interruptions but a unified theater piece."

Hanya recognized the intrinsic humor that waited behind each scene to be discovered and realized in stage terms. It was not a broad humor, but one of utter sophistication, of a benign satire which came about through the transposition of the material. Hanya was fascinated by the satirical element, and it was evident that she loved working on this show. Virgil Thomson said in the *Herald Tribune* that "Miss Holm's design is nothing short of brilliant, especially when it is comic. A burlesque of a South Seas number, entitled 'By Goona-Goona Lagoon' nearly stopped the show last night."

The Golden Apple opened on March 11, 1954, at the Phoenix Theatre. It won the Critics' Circle citation as the best musical of the season and moved from off-Broadway to the Alvin Theatre on the twentieth of April. Hanya was credited for her imaginative choreography, for staging the musical numbers with gusto and inexhaustible fancy. The best proof of her imaginativeness could be seen in the way she handled the figure of Paris. Through movements and dances she had to define his character and establish his position in the play, since he was granted no lines to express himself otherwise. Through Hanya's choreographic design for him he turned into a modern reincarnation of the mischievous and ebullient Paris of Greek legend. "Especially winning and eloquent was his danced response to Helen's singing of *Lazy Afternoon*," Walter Terry wrote. "It was a boyish, teasing dance, for the choreographer would not let us know for certain whether Paris' innocent sensuality was feigned or genuine."

This show received unanimous raves, and most of the kudos fell into Hanya's lap. William Hawkins, reviewing in the New York *World-Telegram and Sun*, exclaimed: "Hanya Holm is a real star of the proceedings. If there was ever a slow moment, it

Photo: Eileen Darby—Graphic House

Photo: Arnold Eagle, by courtesy of Isadora Bennett

9. (a) *My Darlin' Aida.* (b) Choreographers of the New York City Dance Theatre, brought together by Isadora Bennett and Richard Pleasant: Hanya Holm, Charles Weidman, Doris Humphrey; Sophie Maslow, José Limón, Helen Tamiris.

10. (a) *Kiss Me, Kate*: Glen Tetley, Shirley Eckl. (b) *Kiss Me, Kate*.

Photo: Friedman-Abeles

11. *My Fair Lady*, "The Rain In Spain": Julie Andrews, Rex Harrison, Robert Coote.

Photos: Friedman-Abeles

12. (a) *Camelot*, "The Lusty Month of May." (b) *My Fair Lady*, "Loverly": Julie Andrews and Chorus.

is one when everybody went solemn for a line or two, and forgot how vital Miss Holm's inspired dance direction is to the spirit of the show."

If people forgot some of the more remarkable moments of this show, the concept of the warship, a sheer stroke of genius, remained unforgettable to them. There is a scene in the script in which Ulysses and his warriors arrive by boat. Norman Lloyd, the director, had originally planned to have a shell carried across the stage by the warriors. Hanya, however, felt that this realistic bit of stage business would not be in the spirit of the show, and she came up with an idea which was based on movement, was surprising and picturesque, and had the tongue-in-cheek wit that ran through the entire production. She took a bosomy girl and made her up to look like the figurehead on the bow of a vessel. She wore a skirt which was extended into a loop so that a dozen men were within, with the last man leaning backward to supply tension. The feet of Ulysses' warriors were visible, and, walking in a uniform stylized movement, created the feeling of a rocking boat. Then the boat stopped and the immobile girl suddenly turned to the audience. One funny twist followed another.

Leo Lerman, like all the other critics, looked for the right ecstatic expressions without using threadbare superlatives. He wrote in *Dance Magazine:* "It's a lovely, lovely show as far as the dances go, and they go all the way. Pastiche carried throughout an entire evening's entertainment can be very funny: Hanya Holm has managed, in *The Golden Apple,* not only to maintain the fun but to make it into high art."

Reuben, Reuben followed the great success of *The Golden Apple.* It offered challenges of a different nature, posing problems on stage which were psychological as well as purely physical. The show had its own seed of turbulence in its very subject matter. Written by the gifted yet sometimes undisciplined Marc Blitzstein, *Reuben, Reuben* had the appearance of an opera rather than a musical. As a matter of fact, its very definite musical form, with every word being sung, prevented cuts that were needed.

But the handicaps went beyond the risk of destroying the musical form through necessary omissions. The greater complications lay in the fact that it was Marc Blitzstein's own life story and that he had written scenario and music. Being autobiographical, the show lacked esthetic distance. Having been written over a span of five years, it lacked the power of immediacy and remained too close to its creator to live its own artistically valid existence.

The story was concerned with an unbalanced ex-soldier, just discharged from the army, who is alternately swayed by a determination to kill himself by jumping from a Manhattan bridge, and dissuaded from it by his newfound love for a sympathetic Italian girl.

Hanya says, "It was extremely interesting, and I would not have liked to have missed it for anything because there were problems to be solved which had more of a challenge than I had encountered ever before or afterward. Everything in that show and its problems was full of intensity. The story was told in an episodic manner. Marc Blitzstein tried very hard to make his hero overcome his inability to communicate. He went so far as to make him swallow fire. And Eddie Albert, who played this part magnificently, learned to swallow fire. He climbed up the chandelier in a nightclub, thirty feet high, and threatened to jump down. A net of the Fire Department was spread underneath, and it was quite a difficult study to find out how to hold it so that no one should break his arm when he jumped into it. This was the first-act curtain. In the next act he was brought into an insane asylum. I loved to do that scene with all those sane people being insane and the borderline between sanity and insanity blurred. The scene was so powerful that we had the strangest psychological reactions from the audience, shouts like: 'We are insane, Eddie, to have come here, you are not!' That really happened at the Shubert Theatre in Boston."

A beautiful section was the reproduction of the Feast of

San Gennaro, which annually takes place in Mulberry Street. It was one of the highlights of the show, the one point of emotional stability. For the first time there was communication on stage, Marc Blitzstein had created a wonderful scene between a boy and a girl, and in this scene the players strongly communicated with the audience too. "But it did not lift itself into the realm of universality," Hanya says. "Even this scene, which had quite a bit of liberating dancing, remained too much a personal problem with Marc Blitzstein. That was the flaw with book and music which all the power in the story dissipated, that it could not reach out from the personal into the universal, that it never reached the point of being reborn as a work of art. The whole work was self-destructive."

The show folded in Boston, where it had started its tryout on the tenth of October, 1955. It was considered a bore and too pretentious by the critics.

There are people in Leadville, Colorado, and in Denver who still remember the prototypes of the three principal characters in *The Ballad of Baby Doe*. They were Horace Tabor, his wife Augusta, and the beautiful Elizabeth (Baby) Doe.

The events of the story extend from 1880 to 1935. For twenty years the Tabors had no luck. They were sustained by Augusta's skill in cooking and in running a boarding house efficiently. In Leadville the Tabors managed a store. Without Augusta's knowledge — she would probably have disapproved — Horace grubstaked a few miners. One day two of them discovered a rich vein of silver. Within a year the Tabors were millionaires, and Horace went into politics and became mayor of Leadville and later lieutenant governor of Colorado.

His nature was that of an amiable man who could not help being a gambler and spendthrift. Augusta and Horace drifted apart. At the right moment Baby Doe appeared on the scene. She had heard of the famous Tabor and came to Leadville in the hope of meeting him. So she did and, after a quickly arranged divorce, married him. It was her third marriage, and the scandal ruined his political career. The puritanical society of Denver would not accept the bride on any terms.

For ten years they lived happily together and had two daughters. But Tabor remained a reckless spender, and in 1893, when government regulations impoverished the silver-mine owners, Tabor was financially ruined as fast as he had become rich. To the surprise of everyone Baby Doe followed him into his misery as a devoted wife. When he died six years later he made her promise that she would never give up the Matchless Mine which had been the principal source of his wealth. For thirty-six years she endured poverty, and took blow after blow that would have crushed a stronger human being. In the winter of 1935 she was found frozen to death in her hut.

Here was a ready-made tragedy, a piece of Americana with a folksy flavor and an unavoidable touch of sentimentality. Hardly changing the historic facts — the role of Augusta was enlarged for dramaturgic reasons — John Latouche wrote the libretto and Douglas Moore the score. The twenty-fifth anniversary of the Festival of Central City in Colorado was to be celebrated in the summer of 1956. Thus, the Central City Opera House was a "natural" as the place to give this new folk musical play its start. Just as natural was the choice of Hanya Holm as stage director, although this opera required no choreography. But Hanya had just triumphed with *My Fair Lady*, and it was Hanya and her activities in Colorado Springs which had put Colorado on the map artistically. Dr. Edwin Levy, professor in theater at Denver University, was selected as co-director.

Hanya was delighted at having a change of pace from musical comedy. In that medium enchantment and gaiety can be created with elements less complex than those in an opera. On the other hand, *Baby Doe* demanded an intensity and directness of style quite different from grand opera. Hanya immediately realized that, above all, it was important to establish believable theatrical personalities, to set tone and style and maintain them throughout the production.

The opening night, July 7, was a festive event for everyone involved. The local press praised the work as forceful and original. After all, here was a truly American story, here was history relived, here was something familiar to every American. Since *Porgy and Bess* in the thirties no attempt had been made at writing an American folk opera. John Latouche had the right feeling for everything American and so had Douglas Moore. But the story had not the wit and folksy humor of *Porgy and Bess*, nor was the music as rousing and memorable.

Howard Taubman of *The New York Times* was there on opening night and sent this report to his paper:

> This little mining town, 8,000 feet high in the Rockies, which saw bonanza times in the years after the Civil War and which fell into neglect with the decline of its silver, began a steady revival in 1932 with the founding of its festival of drama and music. The Opera House, opened in 1878, was never more refulgent than last night at the premiere of *The Ballad of Baby Doe*. . . .
>
> Taken all in all, *The Ballad of Baby Doe* is a tender, sentimental evocation of the past, with the character of Augusta providing the redeeming bite that gives it dimension as art. . . . Hanya Holm and Edwin Levy have staged the work with gusto and theatrical effectiveness.

Broadway producers were interested in bringing the show to New York, but nothing came of these plans at first. Two years later, the New York City Opera gave this folk opera its New York premiere and has kept it in its repertory. The ways of the world being what they are, particularly the theatrical world, Hanya was not asked to direct the Latouche-Moore opera at the City Center, although the production there remained basically the same. Some changes, however, were made to the detriment of the show. Hanya's comment, accompanied by a shrug of her shoulder, is: "When somebody changes things without knowing why they were done in the first place, naturally they can't have the same impact. It would have been much better to do it entirely differently in New York. Things done haphazardly and half-heartedly in the theater never work."

In 1959 Hanya was invited to stage and choreograph Gluck's *Orpheus and Eurydice* for the Vancouver Festival. She accepted with great anticipation. This was another new challenge. Hanya felt that *Orpheus* was predominantly an opera of choreography. She was fortunate that the principals, Kerstin Meyer and Mary Costa, were not "immobile" singers but were willing to follow the demands of dramatic necessity and were able to express meaning through movement. Most of the dancers had to be chosen from among those living in Vancouver, but it was not too difficult for Hanya to find a capable and cooperative group. Perhaps most important was the fact that, after a couple of rehearsals, they caught the spirit and concept of Hanya's plans and were extremely eager to give all they had.

She tried to re-create a Greek atmosphere without becoming too specific or slavishly imitative of the period. While the chorus did not take part in any stage movement — it stood behind gauze pillars on both sides of the stage — it did comment and advise as well as help convey the mood, which was emotional only in a refined, musical sense.

Donald Oenslager's set dominated the stage and created many problems for the director-choreographer, whose task it became to find artistic compensations for the physical limitations caused by the gigantic, although highly imaginative, sweep of the design which filled the entire stage. The set was as big as a three-story house. It rose sharply at one side to a broad-peaked platform about eighteen feet above the stage level. On the other side it swept downstage in a magnificent parabolic curve of wide, spiraling steps. All this narrowed the stage floor and left only a small strip for the dancers. The many steps were of different heights and different angles.

Although basically Hanya worked with the modern dance idiom, she had a number of ballet-trained dancers and used them to great advantage for a series of difficult lifts. She was able to design a few exciting movements, utilizing the steps, with lifts soaring through the air. The stage set also provided a circular platform halfway up the steps with a hatch that could be swung open. From underneath this hatch covered with a grating, lights came up, a perfect device for the underworld from which the dancers could appear and where they could disappear.

When the Furies confront Orpheus, demanding to know who dares enter their realm, and perform a demonic dance to frighten him, and when he, pleading for mercy, wins them over, the lower world opens for him. Orpheus passes through and the Furies continue their dance. The infernal dance of the Furies was turned into a wild orgy by Hanya. She had costumed these creatures differently and significantly as warriors, traitors, murderers, and insane people, an assortment of beings you would expect to find in hell, and Cerberus had a headpiece with faces on all sides. To underline the wild mood, Hanya had these creatures jump into the hatch head first, which made a strong impression.

The stage set was used imaginatively by Hanya. On the one side where it spiraled upward to sustain the height of the tower, the structure was hollow. She used this hole as the entrance to the tomb in Act One, when Orpheus' well-known lament takes place. But the dancers' expressions projected severity and serenity instead of duplicating Orpheus' lament. The other famous dance scene in this opera is the dance of the Blessed Spirits on the Elysian Fields, with movements light and lively, airy and soaring.

The dancing itself was never Hanya's major problem. It was the merging of music, singers, and dancers, within a relatively short time, into a festive production that would do justice to and illuminate Gluck's eighteenth-century operatic masterpiece, that would live up to Gluck's principle of "grand simplicity."

She met the problem of translating the opera's theme of transcendent love by treating it, as she says, "with a strong simplicity. The lighting became of the higest importance, so that the performers could move in a world created by light and space. All nonessential elements had to be cast out in order to reveal the core, the essence. But such a casting-out process must not impoverish, it must enrich. The complete absence of decoration must not create the feeling of emptiness. The stage must be a resonator that releases every possible nuance of sound, movement, lighting, and action."

The transitions from dance to song were so smooth that they were almost unnoticeable, one of Hanya's fortes which became stage reality at the Vancouver Festival too.

Hanya had great cooperation from the singers. She realized from the very beginning that the director-choreographer must understand what a singer can do as far as movements are concerned. Certain movements are excluded since they would prevent the singer from producing the tone. But not only must the director know what he can expect from the singer, he must also have the good fortune to work with a singer who is willing to step out of the second-position stance. Hanya had just such singers here. Kerstin Meyer had sung the role the previous summer in Drottningholm, Sweden, on the only extant eighteenth-century stage, in a very romantic production. But she adjusted with great skill to what in comparison must have been a totally unromantic approach in Vancouver. To make a singer move, one has first to make clear to him the dramatic points. Hanya encountered no problems with Kerstin Meyer or Mary Costa; as a matter of fact, these two principals sang their last arias from the eighteen-foot-high platform, which must have been physically frightening to them.

"If a choreographer has the musical training and knowledge it is ideal to combine his task with the one of the opera director," Hanya says. "Then dance in an opera is not considered an interlude but a part of the action, as in Gluck's *Orpheus*. In most operas the dance is written into them as relief or incidental happening. Lately choreographers and directors have favored the idea of finding some motivation for these dances. If I choreograph for operas I'd rather direct too. But I fully realize the handicaps and pitfalls. It may be very difficult if you are without the cooperation of the singers. They must feel that you know their problems, that you will not upset any preparation for breath control by using it up for some movement or behaviorism. But there were ways and means to strengthen the dramatic acting of a singer through movement as a part of the director's total concept."

Hanya's double task in staging this opera proved her ability to integrate all theatrical elements. The dancing itself in such scenes as the infernal dance of the Furies or her movement visualizations in the sunlit beauty of the Elysian Fields gave a powerfully dramatic impetus to the production. The lighting — as in *The Ballad of Baby Doe* and in many other shows with which Hanya has been connected — was designed by her son Klaus, who had worked at the Phoenix Theatre for many years and who has become a sought-after lighting expert.

Dancers Henry Kersh of Los Angeles and Maryann de Lichtenberg of West Vancouver were featured in *Orpheus*. The preparations for this production had to be done quickly, as so often in show business, but they were done with Hanya's usual thoroughness. She flew to Oslo, Norway, to see the opera's conductor, Oivin Fjeldstadt. "I had to know if the tempi I wanted for the dances were agreeable to him," Hanya explains. "We went over the whole production many times. We could not afford to have any disagreement when he arrived for the final rehearsals."

Then she traveled to Sweden for talks with contralto Kerstin Meyer, who was to be on stage with the dancers most of the time. "We reached a decision on when she should move and how and whether my conception of her movements was comfortable for her as a singer." Hanya has always found that it is easier to speak about movement to someone who understands music. Built-in awareness of music is essential for dancers as well as singers. Hanya has often pointed out that many professional dancers, including the legendary Anna Pavlova, have had a poorly defined sense of beat; Vaslav Nijinsky was taken to Jaques-Dalcroze to improve his sense of rhythm.

"A sense of rhythm is as important to a dancer as a good technique," Hanya says. "Each individual, whether a dancer or not, has his own individual pace in life. Some are easy-going and slow; others are excitable and do everything 'on the double.' In dancing, personal characteristics must be obliterated. They must give place to only one rhythm — the rhythm of music. The greatest dancers are those who give you the feeling that the music actually flows from them. They do not move on or with the beat. They move in it."

While working with her singers and thirty-two dancers on Gluck's opera, Hanya may not have found the ideal requirements fulfilled in all of them, but she was able to instill in the singers a sense of movement and to make the dancers look like an extension of the music. Howard Taubman, who was dispatched by *The New York Times* to cover the Vancouver Festival, reported on July 19, 1959:

> The production of *Orpheus and Eurydice* . . . was of major league caliber. In its appreciation of Gluck and its freshness of imagination it was worthy of comparison with achievements of the most illustrious competitors in the festival business.
>
> The chief responsibility for the quality of this *Orpheus* devolved on Hanya Holm, stage director and choreographer, and Oivin Fjeldstadt, conductor. To them should go the credit for a memorable accomplishment. Donald Oenslager framed the production in a unit set that consisted of a series of rising levels and that evoked the spirit of Greece in its dignity and simplicity.
>
> Miss Holm's secret was that she avoided literalism . . . Everywhere the movement grew out of the theme of the work. . . . Miss Holm's aim was to capture the basic timelessness of the work, and she carried it off. That she did so was the more remarkable in that her ballet corps was recruited largely from local young dancers with little experience. Some had to be taught how to walk. Nor were the dancers the only members of the cast required to move with plasticity and poetry. The principals were also asked to do so, and they complied.

Hanya repeated her staging of *Orpheus and Eurydice* with a different cast at the O'Keefe Centre in Toronto, Canada, on May 28, 1962.

Experience of life must be channeled into whatever form
of theater.

— HANYA HOLM

Other Media

THEATER is theater, and there is hardly any form
of theater with which Hanya has not familiarized herself, although the musical has remained the field of her major activities, with the opera a perhaps not yet fully fulfilled dream.

Opportunities are not always of one's own choosing. Most
of them come in the course of our response to many questions
and minor challenges; they make themselves felt as the echo
of our own awareness to the very things around us which we
unconsciously help come into existence. Though Hanya had
chosen *The Insect Comedy* as one of the plays that intrigued her
as basic material for a dance drama, she never thought of the
greater ramifications that would follow her production at Colorado College in the summer of 1948. José Ferrer became interested in her college production and made it possible to convert
a semiprofessional performance into a star-studded professional production at the New York City Center the following
fall.

Hanya's concepts about this whimsical Čapek comedy as
worked out with her students in Colorado remained unchanged.
There was an extremely short rehearsal time of only two weeks
to make it ready for the New York opening. Hanya gave José
Ferrer an exact blueprint of what she had done at the College
and the ways in which she desired to repeat or extend certain
ideas. Since Mr. Ferrer was in the first and third acts, Hanya

staged these two acts herself, while he directed the second act, in which he did not appear.

"I was supervising the whole staging," Hanya explains, "and whenever he only slightly departed from the style we had visualized, I pushed him back into it. We worked in the same house, I only had to go to another floor to see whether something had to be straightened out. This is how we achieved a unified show which was convincing and powerful. We also had a few wonderful actors with us who, at that time, were already famous, or who, meanwhile, have become quite well known."

Also in the same year came an incidental job which led Hanya uptown to the Brander Matthews Theatre on the Columbia University campus. Hallie Flanagan Davis, former national director of the Federal Theatre, wrote a play called *E Equals MC²*. It was produced by the Experimental Theatre in June 1948. Miss Davis was one of the originators of the Living Newspaper, which had made a deep impression in the thirties, and in this same style she told everything she knew about the atom bomb. She actually functioned as playwright-compiler-editorialist. There was a trifle of a ballet in the second act which took Hanya three days to choreograph and stage. This production was scheduled for a limited run only.

A year later the New Stages, a group of experimental theater people, produced Federico García Lorca's *Blood Wedding* at New Stages in Bleecker Street. It was a very small stage, somewhat raked, on which Hanya had to work. She referred to it as a "postal stamp stage." Whatever there was in movement, Hanya contributed it. She enjoyed working with the actors and giving this folk-rooted, symbolistic play a very special movement quality. But she saw to it that there was nothing superimposed, that every movement grew logically out of the lines and situations.

The famous Russian director V. E. Meyerhold once wrote, "Words are the design upon the outline of movement. We must put the body back." This was what Hanya did. Movement was in the foreground and extensions of gestures became very expressive. But none of the movement interfered with the play. As Hanya says, "However much you may experiment with movement in a straight play, you must never forget that the play's the thing."

Hanya can easily adjust to all kinds of working methods, even to those in Hollywood. The ways of Hollywood are wondrous. The film producers rarely engage the same stars who were in a successful Broadway show, and hardly ever the same director or choreographer who made a show famous. They have their own mysterious criteria of who has celluloid star qualities, or who can do the right job for them. Hanya, for instance, was not invited to repeat the choreography for the film version of *My Fair Lady*, but neither the director, Moss Hart, nor the star, Julie Andrews, was asked either.

But Hanya got to Hollywood, carried on the wings of her many successes even before her triumph in *My Fair Lady*, particularly her unique contribution to *The Golden Apple*. Someone had the strange notion of reviving an old musical play, a period piece, *The Vagabond King*, which was based on Justin Huntly McCarthy's 1901 work *If I Were King*. Was not *The Golden Apple* a period piece — and successful? Perhaps it was through this tenuous association that Hanya was called to Hollywood to choreograph *The Vagabond King*, which was on stage as far back as 1925 and had been filmed at least twice before. Karl Englund and Noel Langley wrote the new scenario and Rudolf Friml added a few new songs to his old score.

It is a fabricated story with a flamboyant fifteenth-century background in which the rebel poet François Villon plays the leading part. It has always been considered colorful, yet without particular merit. But, as in most cases, Hanya discovered a challenge somewhere to which she could respond. The reaction of the press clearly shows that, however much this filmed operetta was rejected, Hanya's choreography was exempted from all blame. Arthur Weiler wrote in *The New York Times* after the film's opening at the Paramount in Manhattan on September 12, 1956:

> It is no improvement on its predecessors. . . . Hanya Holm, the choreographer, has devised two lively dance sequences. One of these, a play within a play, is an imaginative ballet about Adam and Eve set against a new tune by Rudolf Friml and Johnny Burke titled "Watch out for the Devil." The dancing is more memorable than the music, as is the case in the other number, a boisterous, bouncy item set in a colorful tavern.

Among the many "firsts" which Hanya has to her credit is her appearance on television at a time when its radius was limited to a small section of New York City and the entire medium was still in its earliest infancy. Channel W2XBS broadcast a shortened version of her *Metropolitan Daily* on May 31, 1939, in an hour-long variety program in which Hanya's dance was scheduled between hillbilly singers and Nick Lucas, singing guitarist.

At that time, the dance and television were still strangers to each other. Directors and cameramen had not yet discovered the potentialities of the dance for this medium, the many possible camera tricks, superimpositions, and distortions to create heightened visual effects. No one had had any experience of how to wed the dance to this new electronic medium.

Hanya realized that she was pioneering in this field but that she could do little from a purely technical viewpoint since this was in the hands of the director and the technicians. She knew that in order to achieve the maximum effect she would have to re-choreograph for the camera; as a matter of fact, she was convinced that a transition from staged choreography to televised choreography was basically unsound and that one should rather choreograph something new with an eye for the camera eye. But as far as Channel W2XBS was concerned, the demand was for a transposition of the humorous and successful *Metropolitan Daily* to the television screen.

Hanya reduced the piece to the visually most effective

scenes, always thinking in terms of the limited space, but without basically changing the choreographic design. The television director came to watch several of her rehearsals. Without any precedents of televised dance and with the relatively poor studio equipment at that time — two cameras faced the dancers — one could not expect any fanciful or extraordinary dance creation on the little screen.

But the few hundred people who then had sets and were lucky enough to have good reception were impressed by the straightforward and skillfully composed first television dance. It was only a few years later that people began to recognize the importance of the dance for this mass medium. Then one began to discover the many new possibilities for the teledancers, above all the need for the smooth, rhythmic flow of dance images — which, by the way, Hanya's show achieved to a great extent — the tricky transitions and dissolve shots, the visual motivation for each camera shot in order to achieve unity and coherence.

When Hanya returned to television in October 1957, dance had become one of its major features, and choreographers had great support from experienced directors and better-trained cameramen. NBC planned a one-hour musical-comedy version of the children's classic by C. Collodi about the animated wooden puppet *Pinocchio*. Yasha Frank rewrote the story in condensed form and verses; Alec Wilder was responsible for the music and Hanya for the choreography.

Most viewers and almost all reviewers found the wondrous legend of the wooden puppet a delight and a masterpiece of ingenuity that combined a musical-comedy appeal for adults with a visit to the land of fantasy for the young ones. NBC engaged Mickey Rooney for the part of the impish marionette who finally becomes a real flesh-and-blood boy. It was a difficult part for which Mr. Rooney was an excellent choice. As Papa Geppetto, the cobbler, who carved his son out of a piece of firewood, Walter Slezak had the proper amount of simplicity and wistfulness, and Fran Allison played the blue-haired fairy queen with dignity and airy loveliness. Mata and Hari were seen as marionettes.

The trade paper *Variety* exclaimed: "Miss Holm's choreography and Mata & Hari's execution were topflight, particularly in a puppet sequence and an underwater number . . . lively and delightful entertainment." And John Crosby wrote in the *New York Herald Tribune:* "Wonderfully planned and thoroughly integrated . . . it was a swirl of continuous movement . . . it ended with a big rousing finish with everyone on stage and everyone thoroughly happy, including me." Only Jack Gould of *The New York Times* dissented.

There were a few more experiences, minor in their artistic importance, with the mass media. In the same year in which Hanya worked on *Pinocchio* she was also invited by the Canadian Broadcasting Company to appear as a narrator on *The Dance and the Drama,* one of a series of "Folio" programs. Moreover, Hanya functioned as an assistant writer for this show. In 1963, a dance choreographed for six dancers on the occasion of "Dinner with the President" was televised on a national channel from Washington.

Having traveled in this country and abroad as much as she has, and having had a series of impressive successes with her shows in several parts of the world, Hanya has naturally been invited by innumerable television and radio programs for interviews or for participation on panels and discussion groups. Although she has not always anticipated such invitations with great joy, she has paid the price of popularity and never refused. Being as articulate as she is, she has enjoyed these public exposures in spite of herself. But none of these interviews — and we must also add those in newspapers and magazines to the mass media — was meant to create a personality cult. Some of them, no doubt, promoted a show with which she was identified, a circumstance practically unavoidable. Without ever having had a part in it, she could not help being surrounded by a sea of commercialism. But, in principle, Hanya has always detested self-advertisement.

And she would not be Hanya had she not used such interview opportunities for championing a cause, no matter whether she wanted to hail the accomplishments of the modern dance, to trumpet the triumph of the lyric theater, or only to impress on young and old, on male and female, that physical exercise is a necessity and that obesity goes so easily hand in hand with a sluggish and sloppy mind.

PRINCIPLES AND VIEWPOINTS

The gifted person has the obligation to lead the talented.
— HANYA HOLM

The Dancer

MOST often we embark on learning a craft with certain goals in mind. We want to reach a certain proficiency in order to become whatever our ambition dreams of. Hanya has never determined in advance where and how far a road should lead her. Only once was she very decided in what she wanted in life: she wanted to become a dancer when she saw Mary Wigman perform.

To be a dancer is basic to being a choreographer and teacher. And Hanya worked hard on becoming a good dancer, on achieving a performing skill. There were the apprentice years with Mary Wigman and Hanya's participation in performing and touring with Mary Wigman's company in the twenties. These were Hanya's *Lehrjahre*, in which she learned to master her craft. If she has often been considered by her students as one of the hardest taskmasters among the dance teachers, modern or ballet, then this goes back to her own experiences in those years when she asked the utmost from herself. Above all, she has always demanded to understand what she was doing. She has learned to realize her own limitations, but she also has been willing to push herself to the extreme, to take that one step beyond the possible in order to accomplish her best.

Hanya is fond of telling a story of that early period of her career as a dancer in which she almost brutalized herself to find one of the many keys to knowing. She was practicing turns and circles. She felt she did not yet fully understand the mechanism of the circle, what its impetus was and what would happen if she would let go, not trying to control it. She did let go after running around for two hours, with the result that she hit a wall. She did not mind her bloody and bruised face. The courage to make something go her way, the desire to explore the secret of an unknown why and how, have been indicative of her drive to achieve the utmost. Neglecting the consequences, she could push things to their extreme, and extreme things would happen. Everything became a challenge which she had to dare in order to find out what was behind it. Because if "it" — whatever it may have been — did not work one way, she had to know so that she could try it another way.

From the very beginning Hanya was committed, and the longer she worked with Mary Wigman and helped fashion a whole little world which was the big world of dance for her, the more she became committed. From day to day the world she built for herself began to grow. With uncompromising fanaticism she was student and teacher, still learning by teaching.

Her mind worked to create the foundation for her craft. To know the reasons for what she was doing did not necessarily determine the way her body would move. Her mind worked methodically, but her dancing body could follow the dictates of her sensibility. Her intuitive feelings most often led the way. Whatever she was doing, Hanya could always rely on an inner voice that kept her receptive. Thus, something completely unrelated could influence her and change the course or direction of a thought. But her discipline and strength would not permit her to be sidetracked unless she was willing to give way to a new idea. On the one hand, there has always been this openness and receptivity for the sudden impression from wherever it may have come that protected her from becoming rigid and dogmatic. She never said no to stimuli; she never denied the unexpected. On the other hand, her principles and discipline kept her firmly rooted like a strong tree that liked the wind to play with its branches and in its leaves.

This balance between mind and feelings, between cerebration and intuition, helped her in her creative work. It gave her start as a young dancer the necessary means and ease and became essential for her choreography in later years. Also, working with and learning from Mary Wigman, she became aware of the importance of outside influences and of how to absorb strong experiences without giving up one's personality. She gave herself with utter dedication to the principles of her teacher, but fortunately for her she had joined Mary Wigman at a time when everyone's contribution was decisive. Thus she became a part of the whole, completely engrossed in cooperation toward a great common goal, but a part that also could stand aside and be itself. Mary Wigman saw to it that the spirit of each member of her early group could assert itself. And from that time on Hanya has never surrendered to any outside influences if she has not been convinced of their basic truths and values; but once convinced, she would embrace them wholeheartedly.

Working relentlessly, she reached the technical perfection her body was capable of. She soon realized that you can create movement which is technically correct but not yet dance. She has quite often spoken of her own hard-won experiences when addressing her pupils: "The problem is if you are not technically proficient enough to perform something simple, you try to cover up that deficiency by doing something complicated so that it be exciting enough and worthwhile seeing. But this is not good dancing. It is not necessary to get complicated in order to find something of value. There are simple Czerny exercises for pianists, absolutely composed for the need of dexterity and ease of the fingers. To one person they are just exercises and will sound just like that, but when another person plays them they become beautiful music. In both instances the music was the same. The performance makes the difference."

The human body is composed of many parts. Hanya once compared the dancer's body with an automobile which will take you nowhere until you have all the parts assembled in proper working relationship to one another. If only one part is missing, the car won't move. The dancer must confront herself with all of the "parts" of her profession. Hanya knew that no one could put them together for her, that she had to do it herself, that however much help she received from outside, the ultimate task and responsibility was hers. In those early days she had often thought that what she did was right, and yet she was soon to realize that it did not quite work. Discouraging as those moments were, she would not give in and she started again. She also learned what she was to experience as a dancer and choreographer time and again: when a movement or a phrase was right, it made itself unmistakably felt.

Discoveries were made, gradually, one after the other. She has shared those invaluable experiences with her students. "Emoting is not performing," she says. "You should not appear on stage without the protection of a form. The stage was not created for you as a place to let your emotions flow. Dance is a craft like any other art. The craft is there as a means to an end, but the end result is dance. There are many more craftsmen today than there are dancers. It is much easier to become a craftsman than an artist. You may accomplish the task of bringing the body into the required shape and form, but then there is no feeling yet, the dynamics are missing. Briefly, there is no art, there is nothing but craftsmanship. The craftsman and the artist are two worlds apart. If you stay only a rhymer, then rhyme as well as you can but don't call yourself a poet. If you are basically a good technician and nothing else, then it would be dishonest to pass yourself off as an artist."

A great deal could be said about the long and arduous growth of a dancer. Her education, which takes all hours of the day, not only challenges the body but also the dancer's personality. In the mirror of her physical metamorphosis one can see her inner changes, and, in turn, her mental changes become mirrored in the growing visual image of her as a dancer. In Hanya's case her constantly rising ability to master all technical aspects to find the best possible modulation of her body went hand in hand with her increasing capacity for teaching the experiences of her own body. One complemented and furthered the other. The teacher in Hanya helped the dancer in her to greater awareness.

Hanya danced many parts in Mary Wigman's company throughout the twenties, smaller and bigger parts in the group works, culminating in the second most important role in *Das Totenmal* in 1930. She developed into one of the most reliable co-workers Mary Wigman could wish for, one who could be trusted with every job that needed to be done in the studio or on stage.

In appearance she was a determined, energetic person, petite, with fair skin and blond hair. There was a distinct delicacy and an expressive lyricism in her dancing from the very beginning. She was different from dark-haired Mary Wigman, whose dynamic nature put other and dramatically stronger accents on the art. Hanya developed an impressive fleetness, a strikingly quick footwork, lightness on the floor and when lifted. One of the surprising features of her dancing was the uncanny strength and drive she displayed, which in no way contradicted her lyricism. In spite of this marked intensity, her way of moving remained more often than not cool, as if the dancer would try to stay away from too much personal involvement.

What also distinguished Hanya's dancing was her intimate relationship to music, which strongly motivated her. Her early music training was the best preparation for the career she chose. She had her first great bout with music when, in 1929, she was chosen to dance the role of the Princess in Stravinsky's *L'Histoire du Soldat*, her first major solo part. She had to find a way of getting behind the unusual, almost unwieldy rhythms to wed the conception and manner of her dance to the accompaniment. She buried herself in it for hours and days until she was able to feel the pulse of the music without having to count it, until she had the feeling of having conquered all insecurities as to measured time-space and space-time relationship. Finally, having learned to *feel* the music, she felt safe in her performance, which turned out to be a great success. One year later her participation as a dancer in *Das Totenmal* established her as one of the modern dancers in Germany whose future career seemed assured.

But Hanya arranged another fate for herself when she decided to leave Germany and her past achievements behind her. When she came to New York as the director of the Mary Wigman School she was fully aware that she had come in the role of a teacher, not as a performing artist. And teach she did. Moreover, during Hanya's first season in New York Mary Wigman was on her second transcontinental solo tour, which repeated her success of the previous year and took the spotlight from Hanya.

Hanya realized that any attempt on her part to push her chances as a dancer would have been detrimental to her success with the Wigman School. Nor did Sol Hurok's offer to put together a company, which he was ready to send on tour, distract her from her task as she saw it. With single-minded determination she worked on keeping the school afloat and on gradually forming a company. Not until 1936, when Hanya's company and her first program were ready to be shown, did she appear publicly on stage with her group.

When she was first seen in America as a choreographer and dancer, she had been known as a teacher for several years. It was inevitable that her choreography for her group should be judged separately from her performance as a dancer-choreographer. John Martin saw her in Bennington in the summer of 1936. He reported in *The New York Times:*

> In her personal dancing Miss Holm has not yet made the same strides toward a new goal that she has made in her group work. It is still too small in its dimensions to be effective in the theatre. Though her style is naturally delicate and intimate, it needs further brightening of color, sharpening of projection, heightening of climax. She knows the stuff of movement, however, as if by instinct, is never guilty of mere invention, and when she has

attained a greater drive her dancing will be extremely eloquent and moving. Already these qualities are present in essence.

Some critics realized that after so many years Hanya had decided to dance again in public primarily to provide a focus for the dancing of her group. She herself would have been the first to admit that the total effect of her group was far more important than her own solo dancing. Some of the early members of her group recalled that Hanya very skillfully cast herself in central dramatic roles in such a manner that substantial parts of the dance would revolve around her, with the dancers moving toward her, and she herself would hold the spotlight through intensity.

"Hanya's importance to the American dance scene — and she is very much a part of it — is that she is one of the founders and formers of the American modern dance, beginning with Isadora, Ruth and Ted, but in her generation belonging with Martha, Doris, Charles and Helen. I think Hanya belongs right there," Walter Terry stresses. "Graham was the greatest performer in that generation. Hanya's least gift was as a performer, but I don't say as a technician or dancer because nothing was sloppy about her dancing at all. I speak in terms of impact. Well, a blond has a much harder time than a brunette."

Alwin Nikolais feels that Hanya never was a great performer and thinks that Hanya would agree. He says that she had to rely on her good choreography to entice an audience; that although her dances were very beautiful and she had dancers of star quality with her, her performances lacked the glamorous aura of a Graham.

It seems that anyone looking back to the late thirties cannot help but orient his perspective from the viewpoint of Martha's dazzling performance. Hanya has never thought in terms of competition. Having decided on other tasks as being more important to her and to the cause of the modern dance, particularly to further the Mary Wigman concepts, she thought little of developing and testing her performing skill. But, as Walter Terry intimated, we must discriminate between performing and dancing skill. The latter was never doubted. Hanya's self-criticism forced upon her a technical proficiency which did not tolerate weaknesses and compromises. It is to her credit that she recognized that her ultimate potentialities lay in other fields. If the modern dance lost an important performer in her, it gained an unsurpassed teacher and a choreographer of stature.

In one of his Sunday columns — on February 26, 1939 — John Martin summarized his personal observations about Hanya at that time of her career and wrote with foresight about her:

> Hanya Holm is a master of the subject of movement not only for herself but for others. This latter consideration is of great moment to her, for she is in no sense a "star" dancer; in all her compositions she is only one of several soloists, and the main emphasis is upon the group as a whole. Though some of her girls move better than others, the general standard is remarkably high, and the movement itself is a revelation of what dance movement can be. It is none of your tentative, hit-or-miss systems, but in its every manifestation is activated by a central principle. Nor is this an arbitrary or stereotyped principle, but that upon which the body itself is designed to move. Call it "natural" movement, if you will, for no matter how far it departs from the actual practices of life movement, how much it employs the formalizations and distortions which are necessarily involved in the making of art, it retains always a clear sense of the normal body.
>
> It is, to be sure, without set vocabulary, and ranges freely in response to inner direction, always with authority because so closely related to natural function. There is no strain or forcing even where the higher reaches of dynamics are involved, and at the opposite end of the scale it makes skillful use of small and delicate material. Here is movement of beautiful balance because expertly produced; in short, the ideal stuff of which the dance is made.

> Do not escape, get drunk on a sensation of the body! God
> is not in you if you are not "it."
>
> — HANYA HOLM

The Choreographer

JOHN MARTIN ended his February 26, 1939, article
with two paragraphs:

> In the matter of composition Miss Holm works with equal
> fluency. Though like all artists she has a personal idiom, she has
> a faculty for evolving creative material out of experience, and
> apparently for eliciting the same kind of thing from her group.
> Beyond this purely personal material, however, she has an intui-
> tive sense of the scene as a whole, and hits upon remarkable bits
> of counterpoint and moments of secondary accent to support her
> major theme. As a natural consequence there is always mood
> and atmosphere to what she does, and frequently a highly dra-
> matic color, even though the movement is not in itself intense.
> It is obviously clear to her that other things are dramatic be-
> sides screaming at the top of one's lungs, so to speak.
>
> Because she is keenly aware of the part that space plays in the
> work of the dancer, her compositions not only possess the emo-
> tional enrichment which this knowledge gives to any movement
> but also work consistently in three physical dimensions. They are
> never flat and proscenium-conscious, but make use of the full
> depth of the space at their disposal. Indeed, Miss Holm uses the
> stage extraordinarily well both spatially and in the more conven-
> tional theatrical sense.

This explains astutely a great many features of Hanya's
choreographic approach, particularly as seen from a viewer's
or reviewer's aisle seat. One of her primary objectives is purity,
a clean style. To achieve this, she strips away all artificialities,
trying to keep close to life. "The thing that makes a rose to be a

rose is its fragrance," she says. "Man can make beautiful glass flowers like the ones in the museum of Harvard University in Cambridge, they are almost lifelike. Only the fragrance is missing. This cannot be made artificially."

Hanya's choreography is organically developed. She would not think of progressing to a new point without being certain that her progress is exactly right and that it is what she wants. She could easily spend four hours on ten seconds of work, in the days when she worked in the concert field. Of course, the pressures of the Broadway "business" dictate a different time measure. But in neither case would she suffer any slovenly procedure in her craft. If gestures have to be at a certain point of space and time, she insists on their being there. She will not tolerate wrong notes any more than a musician would.

Her inspired intuition in movement encompasses the scene as a whole, as John Martin indicated, but her meticulous procedure does not neglect any single detail. She draws her strength from her intuitive capacity when creatively active, and at the same time she can rely on her extremely logical mind, which has been variously described by her students and co-workers as "brilliant," a mind of "great intelligence and integrity," "a critical mind which can be merciless toward anyone as well as toward herself." Hanya can easily spot a mistake or flaw in any dance work and, with logical sharpness, she can pinpoint and verbalize anything that needs attention and repair. The same keen eye is on the alert where her own creative efforts are concerned. It is then difficult to say whether intuition or logic helped her catch a "wrong move," since both are equally strong and constantly on guard.

After she had to give up her company, she faced the problem of translating other people's ideas into her idiom. Since she had always been strongly inclined toward the theater — even the concert stage was nothing but a platform for a theatrical experience to her — it became clear that she could work with plays very well. She sees a musical, an opera, or a straight play from the viewpoint of its stage images. She seems to have a built-in sense that tells her what can work on stage and what cannot. Hanya is able to inject or to identify with humor as easily as with a tragic quality, she can read into the lines what the author may have left unsaid. She interprets music in her own special way, never following its pattern or melody, rather drawing from it an idea which turns into a guiding rod; she lets music permeate her entire being, and only when she is certain that it has become a part of her is she ready to give it its movement quality. Whatever the work may be, she puts the signature of her personality upon it without trying to dominate the scene. She has often stressed that a stage work can succeed only when no one of the collaborating egos wants to impose its will.

Within a very few years' work with her own group in the thirties, Hanya's personality as a choreographer became strongly defined and easily recognizable. Walter Terry wrote in 1940 that "the name Holm has come to signify a style of dance joyful in spirit, broad in range of movement and almost faultless in technical execution." He was particularly impressed by how truly feminine were her dancers, who simply were not afraid of being graceful.

John Martin stressed in several of his articles that Hanya never choreographed for herself as a soloist to further her ego but to integrate her role in the theme of the dance. He recognized the tremendous care with which she shaped an ensemble, with each of her dancers harmoniously attuned to the quality of the whole group. "Miss Holm," he wrote, "always an expert in developing dancers that can move, has built up an ensemble that is not only technically excellent, but also has a flavor all its own. This is not altogether a technical matter, to be sure, but owes a great deal to its leader's unusual ability to choreograph for a group."

Hanya has always watched carefully the quality of each instrument at her choreographic disposal. She has an uncanny sense for how much she can get out of a dancer and how to turn existing weaknesses into apparent fortes. Above all, she has always tried to make each dancer understand what he was doing or what he was supposed to do. It is never a matter of technique with her, of speed, dynamics, or projection only. The main idea is to make the intent of the movement come across.

Some advice given to the students of one of her composition classes sheds light on her approach as a choreographer: "You may have wonderful ideas for choreography but it may happen that you cannot get out of the dancers what you want them to do, no matter how hard you try. You will have to set back your demands and make them according to what your people can give you. This means that you can't choreograph as you would like but you choreograph according to the material you have to work with. This can be fatal. It can also be good, depending on how intelligently you meet the dancers half way."

Hanya has always strongly believed in the importance of the individual dancer and his very personal contribution to a work. After all, the choreographer can only devise certain concepts and ideas, she can visualize movement patterns and imagery in the minutest detail, but she always depends on the understanding, technical skill, and physical make-up of the dancer who is to carry out and project her visualizations. Hanya never tries to impose her will on her dancers, she does not want to have puppets on stage but dancers, attuned to her concepts by way of understanding and sense perception. "She has great respect for personality," Walter Terry says. "She does not want to have a lot of little Hanyas, imitations, but the best from everyone."

This method begins in her classroom. Alwin Nikolais tells of his own experiences with Hanya as a teacher and choreographer: "Besides the technique class we had lessons of exploration of a particular principle taught in the technique class. What was first a principle of motion became a challenge in the theory class, a challenge which, pursued by the dancer through improvisation or other means, turned into his own concept of that particular principle. This, in turn, led to the development of the dancer as an individual and gave him the opportunity of personal exploration.

Photo: Marshall Brooks

13. (a) *Orpheus and Eurydice*, Underworld scene, in performance.
(b) *Orpheus and Eurydice*, in rehearsal.

14. (a) The Hanya Holm School: An Exercise in Dance Notation.
(b) Teacher and Student: Alice Reyes, Hanya Holm, at Colorado College, 1968.

15. The Hanya Holm School: An Exercise in Percussion.

Photo: © Arnold Newman

16. Mother and Son, the 1960s: Hanya Holm and Klaus.

"Well, when it comes to choreography the method also applies in a similar manner, and legitimately so. For example, when Hanya was working on a particular subject she would frequently ask the dancers to improvise on the subject and she would spot the interesting aspects the individual dancer might come up with. Once recognizing these aspects, she would hold onto them, remake them, or develop them from that point into her choreography."

Sometimes misunderstandings and difficulties have arisen from this method. Some dancers are under the impression that, in effect, they are doing the choreography. But this is not so, because Hanya comes to the rehearsal with a preconceived notion of a certain subject matter — however general in outline this notion may be — and it is always Hanya who makes the selections from the resulting improvisations and determines how and where certain steps should be used. In other words, it is Hanya who brings with her the idea of what should go into a dance number, but she tries to find the dancer's physical peculiarities and strengths and to use them to best advantage. It is also important for her to have the dancer thus display the areas he or she is best suited for. Then the selections are made and the material developed by the choreographer.

This method is very important for choreographing solo parts in musicals. Hanya watches the particular attributes of a soloist and then tries to find a range of movement to suit that particular body. When dancers are engaged for musicals, Hanya can often select from among those whose abilities she knows and who are well adjusted to her working method. But the intimate and stimulating collaboration that existed as long as Hanya had her own company is not found on Broadway, where there are always newcomers and where there are constant pressures and harassments. Hanya has taken the Broadway conditions in her stride and, more often than not, has had a harmonious working relationship with her cast.

"You should always have some pretty definite idea in mind before you begin to search for movement," Hanya tells her class. "There are several ways of finding movement. But your original idea must remain the angle from which you make your selection. One thing is essential: to find movement you have to keep yourself in an emotional stage of motion."

Hanya is never able to embark on a new artistic enterprise in which she cannot wholeheartedly believe. She must feel its relation to life. It must have the pulsebeat of something she knows or can well imagine. She once told an interviewer: "I watch people in their daily role — in life apart from the stage. Their emotions, actions, and reactions, at ease and under fire, all are noted. I absorb, then translate into dance."

I told her that taking classes with her has made me understand myself better and adapt myself more easily; that I've learned to measure myself, to master other problems in other fields; that I was able to have a leash on myself. She was very pleased and said that, beyond making dancers, she wanted to make a person out of each student, one who knows himself and who is not afraid of saying: This is me!

— FROM AN INTERVIEW *with*
one of Hanya's students

The Teacher

BY 1937, about six years after Hanya's arrival in New York, it had become common knowledge in dance circles that she was an excellent teacher. When Walter Terry, at that time writing for the *Boston Herald,* entitled his critique of Hanya's first program, "Importance of Hanya Holm: A GREAT TEACHER," he was only echoing what dancers already knew. He wrote: "Hanya Holm must be a great teacher, for the members of her group actually dance. They follow her choreography, they conform to the manner in which she wants an idea to be expressed, but each of them has an individual quality of movement. . . . Ask most modern dancers to get up and dance for the sheer love of movement; they look a bit blank and ask you to state a theme or tell what kind of movement you want. But it is a safe bet to say that Hanya Holm's girls would be able to dance at a moment's notice, for their teacher has taught them more than the mechanics of movement — she has taught them the essence and the spirit of dancing."

To impart the essence and the spirit of dancing is, to this very day, the mainspring of her teaching. Granting the expansion of her ideas, the development of a maturing mind, and an accumulation of experience in a new environment, the approach and the basic concepts have remained what they were. To her, teaching is a most creative process, another aspect of the artist's life. Teaching means going back to her roots. It is not important to her how many pupils she has, but how far beyond the familiar she can reach and how much she can give, because she has always realized that in helping to form others you are forming yourself.

The artist, seeking as he does the creative expression of contemporary ideas and ideals as the spokesman for his time, needs the necessary tools, knowledge and inspiration. His language is movement and his medium the body. Hanya stresses natural movement based on what the human body is structurally capable of doing. As a teacher she sees to it that the pupil realizes from where the movement stems, why he does what he does and why he ought to do it that way. "I never make a student do something," Hanya says. "I try to make him understand what I mean, and then I want him to do it as if it were his own idea, because, after all, he must carry it and make it succeed."

Typical of comments by students who have worked with her are: "Hanya really digs in and makes you aware of where movement comes from." "Her method is clean, based on essences of movement rather than a personal idea of technique." "Her classes are always so beautiful. There is a progression in the teaching of each class she teaches that makes every session a work of art." "Her classes are unusually integrated, everything is built up and related from beginning to end." "Not what you do matters with her, but how you do it."

About a dance symposium Hanya had been teaching at Adelphi College in 1954, a colleague said: "From the first apparently unrelated strands through a gradual drawing together of the materials she achieves a final delineation of the specific theme which emphasizes with power and clarity the consistent point of the entire lesson."

While other teachers may give their pupils something personalized, her ideas are based on universal facts, on the intrinsic nature of movement. She sees as the teacher's major task the opening of many new vistas; she tries to assist the student in finding the full realization of his self, in developing into whatever direction his own impulse, his own creative energy leads. To Hanya, some of the tenets for a dance teacher are:

"First, she should herself be a person of artistic sensibilities, an artist in spirit if not in finished achievement; second, her training should be along lines of artistic integrity with the highest standards of accomplishment and towards a firm understanding of the fundamental nature of art in general and of her chosen medium in particular."

Hanya believes that in all human beings — whether they want to become dancers or not — should be awakened the feeling for the beautiful, because even a movement as prosaic as walking can become a thing of beauty if done well. And the beautiful movement must also be the most efficient.

Hanya's technical demands are strict, and what she asks from her students, as well as from the artists she works with, she has earned the right to ask through the rigorous requirements she had always imposed upon herself: no mechanization, no superimposed feelings, but a oneness in the performer and accuracy and precision in movement.

Her demands, being as great as they are, find various student reactions according to the degree of the students' seriousness and devotion to the art. In spite of the fact that she is a perfectionist, she does not expect you to reach perfection within an undue period of time. She makes you feel that you may achieve it, but only if you work on yourself hard enough with the necessary understanding of what you are doing. She gives you time to find your own limitations and possibilities. She helps you see what suits you best so that, in your own particular way, you can achieve fullest development.

Hanya's technique, theory, and composition classes cannot be isolated from each other. All three are closely interrelated in a whole viewpoint on teaching. Although Hanya's technique has certain routines of action which are very exact guidelines to movement, they are only a part of a much larger scheme in which the logic of these particular things is applied to movement generally. Her technique is basically oriented into space and direction, and it makes a clean, pure, and clearly analyzed impression. It covers a huge range of movement experience, including almost anything the body is capable of doing without being forced into any formal codification.

When the figure is standing still, the body and its parts have all kinds of directional relationships in depth, width, and height to the space surrounding it. When the figure travels in space, the directional relationships of the body and its parts are compounded by the body's directional path in space. What sets her theory apart from all other techniques is the expansiveness she achieves with the outward direction of the body.

There is a continually flowing feeling in her highly objective use of the dancing body in space, giving it unlimited freedom. With weight placement in forward direction, the body cannot help but move and attain a searching quality, the sensation of never being at rest, of having to keep the movement alive. Only the ancient Greeks knew of such activity of motion which gives the body the means to unfold. Watching Hanya's dancers move, you are under the impression that what they are doing has a feeling of radiation, of growing through time and into space as if aspiring to something unattainable.

But what Hanya wishes to achieve in a technique class is very specific. Bessie Schönberg once found the best descriptive phrase for it when she said that Hanya "picks it to the bone." She goes down to the core of the material and makes the student work at it, which is disciplinary and often difficult to achieve, yet intellectually comprehensive. What she sets up in the technique class she uses in the theory and composition classes, where the student is allowed to experiment and to expand within certain limitations. This procedure is most valuable for all creatively inclined people.

Of course, there are technical rules, specific movements which she has codified. For instance, when you are on a diagonal you can't be half way in between — you are specifically forward or backward, rotating or doing spiral action. If you are doing falls, then you are falling in a very specific way. If you are working on a diagonal problem in the technique class, you may further explore in the theory class what diagonals have to offer in space, what they mean to your hips and chest, to head, torso, and legs.

The important question in the composition class is how you evolve your material from the idea that is presented; whether the form which is based on the nature of your material fits the idea.

Usually Hanya does not apply any system; she simply improvises as she goes along according to what she considers the needs of the group that confronts her. Alwin Nikolais remembers that she would present a challenge or a problem to her students, who would then work on it and submit the result to her criticism. He pictures her extraordinary perception and sharpness in criticizing a wide range of material, her capacity for seeing the esthetic value in whatever was done by the students because she was not particularly anchored in any specific area of thought. But since she has such a sharp eye, her criticism is usually detailed and thus often creates the feeling among the students that one can never do anything right.

"However, this did not mean that her classes were not enjoyable," Alwin Nikolais says. "You certainly learned a great deal and yet not in the patterned sense. There was no formula for doing things, you were simply challenged, you could choose your subject within that area of challenge and then go at it. Hanya would look at it and give her impressions of the result. When finally you did something that she considered an accomplishment of the problem, you were greatly elated because you had the confidence that the stamp of approval really carried some meaning. Dancers prominent in the field would often come to Hanya for criticism on their dances, take her critique very seriously, redo and revamp their work."

Hanya's ability to verbalize her thoughts, often in vivid language, tempts her to teach a great deal by talking. If the student is very much interested in dance and also in her as a teacher, he can profit just by listening to her explanations and exhortations. Although she is inclined to overexemplify, never being quite sure she has really been understood, she may not comment for days after one of her detailed critiques, so that meanwhile the student can put to use what she has said. Excepting certain explanations which accompany her teaching and are usually kept proportionately brief, she can be provoked into longer diatribes by anger or seeming helplessness over the students' inability "to get a point." If this happens, I have observed that Hanya will then talk for the rest of the hour and give the class a tongue-lashing which may puzzle some and upset others. The weak will be discouraged, the strong will grow on such castigation.

Hanya brings to her teaching a *Weltanschauung*, a whole philosophy of life, for which her verbalization is one of the more important outlets. Her examples from other fields of artistic activity, the analogies from her personal experiences, document and illustrate her points. She can cajole with innuendoes and be brutally frank with hard-hitting similes. From the beginning Hanya tries to relate to the students, to hold up an ideal mirror image of a dancer, to help overcome impediments and shortcomings.

Her comments are an impassioned reasoning with her students. She wants to give her dancers the necessary insight into her ideas. She tries to free the body from constrained and meaningless habitual movements, from inertia, and to transform it into an instrument responsive to the demands of the living personality. The body must become an exquisitely sensitive instrument in its knowledge of form, in its search for expression. The actual physical training of the body and the creative development of the personality must go hand in hand. The particular value of the dance as an educational medium lies in the very fact that it provides a simultaneous development in the physical and psychological faculties of the student.

Her method relies on natural movement; that is, movement based on the structural and functional capabilities of the human body and the generally controlling factors of time, space, and energy. There is an awakening period whose purpose is to co-ordinate and develop the functions of the body — the functions of the muscles, joints, and organs of breathing — to a point where the body will no longer stand in the way of the expression of an idea, a mood, or an experience. This training is both general and flexible in its approach, it does not aim at the development of a "style" of movement copied after any one dancer or teacher but at the discovery of the universal truths of movement without which one cannot hope to reach truth in feeling and expression.

Her initial approach to creative dance usually is through the medium of improvisation. The student is encouraged to express through movement the spontaneous impression caused by a suggestion in music, mood, or imagination. Thus, habits and inhibitions that stifle the desire for self-expression are gradually thrown off. Above all, the student learns that he must have something to say and that his expression will not be clear if he uses borrowed phrases. A step and gesture carry no conviction unless they are true to the idea and personality expressing the idea. In this way the hard lessons of simplicity and truth are learned and sometimes mastered. The imagination is stimulated, and the inescapable and subtle relations of form and idea are slowly experienced and realized; so are the natural dynamics of movement, intensity, shift of accents, projection into the spatial significance of movement or into a physical response to a mood, and so forth.

John Martin saw the value of Hanya's method, saying, "More important than any mere additions to the repertory is the emergence among us of a fundamental art, so free, so sound and so inspiring as Miss Holm's." And Walter Terry wrote: "Her principles of dance and her application of these principles in terms of American dancers is for our country her great single contribution and one which goes even beyond her own classroom work itself. . . . I like her for her openness to new ideas, absorbing, digesting and giving them focus and new life in terms of her own particular skills as a teacher." Margaret Lloyd added her voice to those who realized the importance of Hanya as a teacher after having observed her technique classes in Bennington:

> Miss Holm is known as a superlatively fine teacher, who makes technique interesting without sparing the rod of rigorous training. She builds logically from the simple scales of movement to the more complicated exercise. Beginning with the whole body as the nucleus, she works out specific details in ascending degrees. There is endless variety as well as endless repetition in this method. At Bennington I watched her with one of her classes, devoting an hour to feet. The class began with flexing them, in various positions acquiring balance on them, and finally, through sequences of multiple shadings, ending in a crescendo of thrilling turns on them.

Today her great contribution as an influence, as a teacher, has become incontestable. Both John Martin and Walter Terry agree that besides the important role she has played in the development of the modern dance as a teacher and choreographer, she also influenced the ballet, particularly in the forties when there was still a rift between the modern dance and the *danse d'école*. Hanya healed that breach by teaching ballet dancers "not to become modern dancers," as Walter Terry says, "but how to *be* dancers. They could go into a classical, a Jerome Robbins or Antony Tudor ballet and be better for having studied with Hanya the principles of movement." The classically trained ballet dancers found her technique, the principles of her neoclassicism, congenial. These dancers recognized that Hanya's principles extended their understanding of ballet and gave them greater fluidity and mobility in action.

Also, there is a long list of prominent actors, among them José Ferrer, Uta Hagen, Gene Nelson, Martha Wright, and Fritz Weaver, who at one time or another have worked with her and reaped the benefit of understanding the truths of movement. What Hanya looks for in a talent is a heightened sensitivity and receptivity to experience without necessarily becoming a dancer and, furthermore, the ability to externalize this inner experience in a vivid and permanent art form.

Her group lecture-demonstrations in the thirties propagated the modern dance. It was extraordinary pioneer work which helped make America more dance-conscious. With her summer headquarters in Colorado College, she stimulated art activities in the West. Hanya has also acted as consultant professor of the Dance Department at Adelphi College. She has lectured, taught, and demonstrated at more than sixty colleges and universities, creating real interest and helping tremendously to expand the scope of dance in physical education departments into channels of artistic thinking. Also, many of her students and co-workers have brought Hanya's methods into colleges and universities throughout the country. From them new generations grow up with concepts flowing from the richness of her roots.

Hanya has always wanted her pupils not only to know how to dance, but also to have something to dance about. She insisted that her dancers must break out of their own limited circle and widen their horizon in every respect. In the early thirties, she was the first to stress the interrelation of the various subject areas. Thus, she offered a course in anatomy; she initiated percussion training so that the students could develop a more advanced kinesthetic response to rhythm than what could be incidentally experienced during the classes. For some time John Martin taught history of the dance and afforded better insight in the social function of the dance, its historic background and relation to the other arts. Hanya is strongly committed to Labanotation. Not only was she the first in this country to record her own choreography, it was part of the curriculum in her school. Hanya has also brought to her teaching her wonderful background of music training — which, by the way, has been appreciated by the many musicians and composers who have worked with her.

Hanya is a dancer who teaches because there are certain things the dancer can give but not the teacher. "That word 'teacher' has an awful connotation," Hanya says. "If there is anything in life I am proud of having achieved it is being a dance educator. If for no other reason than the one that the sacrifice was too great. Who knows about the lonely road I had to take, the deep understanding I had to gather, the utter devotion with which I lived for it. If that isn't religion, then I do not know what religion is."

For her teaching has never been only a matter of a few steps or stretches, the technique of this or that. This has been part and parcel of the information and training, but it is not all. True, there has always been that imaginative something that has made even technique appear like a living experience. But there is still more to it. Perhaps it is the ability to select and analyze or to look into a human being and recognize his hopes, dreams, fears, and weaknesses. And then, moreover, there is her so often mentioned philosophy of life, an outlook which impresses so many and which creeps into her teaching time and again. Some have said that her classes center around a Jungian viewpoint, and most students and observers agree that she teaches a rather scientific and basic kind of dance which makes great sense in terms of a psycho-physiological union, a union of body and mind. And yet there is still more to it.

In her role as a teacher she has reached far above all this into a realm where one no longer can say: Oh, you taught me this! An intoxicating stimulant has got hold of the student, the spark of creativity which ignited something in him that cannot be named or explained. This inexplicable thing may easily derive from the dancer in the teacher and more so from the inner power which may be in all of us but which Hanya, the teacher, can unleash and creatively set free. An almost mystical feeling emanates from this power that is awareness, part of it an awareness of space which is everywhere and only limited when she herself puts limitations to it. And within this space her students move, surrounded by a thousand and one possibilities. The lucky ones, those willing and able, catch her vibrancy.

"I don't want to put myself above anyone else," Hanya says, "but I am not a teacher in the ordinary sense of the word. And this is one thing I do care about. I know there is something behind it, but I don't know whether I will ever be able to make it clear, to verbalize it. It is something you cannot classify or categorize. If I could predict what will be tomorrow I would stop functioning. But there is a force there, a power, something inevitable whose nature and source I do not understand. If it were no longer there, if I could not reach out for it, I would have lost a personal secret."

Hanya Speaks

You are your own master and student. There is no value in copying what someone else has done. You must search within your own body. What you discover there will be for your own benefit. Others can give you the means, the tools, but they cannot do it for you. The art of dancing is in no book, nor can you take it with a spoon or in form of pills. Dance can only result from your own concentration and understanding. When you do stretches, sit-up exercises, or whatever you may be doing, you are doing it for one purpose only: you want to make an instrument out of what is otherwise a mere body.

There is a difference between acting a movement and actually doing it. In the final analysis it is meaningless to count the amount of jumps you can do, because one small gesture which is right and proves the oneness of purpose in what is being done will far outweigh everything else.

Finding something is the greatest thing that can happen to you. If you are searching you will make new discoveries, but searching is not easy. You cannot help facing movement blocks that will stand in your way. No one can remove these blocks except you yourself, and only when you are able to remove them will you eventually discover yourself. This is the only way you can improve and grow into something big.

You need an enormous amount of inspiration within yourself. Don't wait for someone to light a candle within you or place a bomb under you. A bomb causes external excitement which is quite the opposite from the excitement you should have. The excitement must come from your inner focus. There can be no inner focus if you are not aware of what the head is doing, what the arm, the trunk, the back is doing. The entire body must be knowledgeable before there can be an inner focus. The same moment you discover that focus you will burst forth in your outward appearance. Your audience will recognize it immediately. The people won't have to look inside of you for emotional overtones. Your chest will be right, your hip will be right, you will have a carriage that is supported and that is right for that which is intended.

Let's face it, the art of dance is much bigger than any one of us. We are ants in relation to what dance is, but it is an honor to be that ant. Don't say, "Oh well, we did that, and I kicked my leg five inches higher than she did." Who cares? Did you understand the movement? That is what matters.

Don't swallow everything hook, line, and sinker. Absorb! React! There isn't such a thing as *"the"* gospel. Don't expect a compliment unless you deserve it. When you do receive a compliment take it at its face value. Good dance instructors do not throw around compliments. They don't throw them away. If you are dissatisfied because of lack of praise, see why you are dissatisfied. Is it the teacher's fault or yours? Your enemies are not those about you in the studio, but your own imperfections. You can't fight yourself if you run away and refuse to see yourself.

On stage there is no use pretending you are an ostrich with your head in the sand. The audience recognizes everything you are trying to hide. Every gesture you make reveals something of you. Don't think you can hide behind a gimmick, or a little bit of extravaganza you have learned to master with great flourish. Even the simplest movement will be marvelous if it is fullfilled by you, by your real self. When you dance you are naked.

> There is no easy short cut to learning how to dance. Don't walk around lamenting that you "didn't feel right, or you didn't feel this or that, or the movement wasn't right for you, or you were out late last night." You have no excuse. You must function right there where the demand is made. Your whole life with its ups and downs must be focused. This doesn't mean that you have to live like a bird in a cage. On the contrary, open up and fly out. That little magnet in the center holds you together. Master whatever comes your way and enjoy the mastering. Unless you are challenged there is no work, there is no accomplishment, there is nothing of value, there is no test of your strength. Strength has to be challenged, otherwise it is lost. Challenges are just as important to life as eating, perhaps even more so.

Watch little children when they hear some music. They throw themselves around and onto the floor and jump up again. They don't get hurt. They don't care. They enjoy it. They fall down a second time and roll over and laugh it off. You should be able to do the same thing but you kill it with fear. They have no fear. Art is living. It is not just craftsmanship. It is the flow of love. There is that meeting place of the body and the soul and the spirit that gives you control.

> A walk is of no value unless it is of the nature that you can change it. You should be able to do an angry walk, a floating walk, a sombre walk, a determined walk cutting into space. You must be able to change it to fulfill the inner demand of

what you want the walk to be. If you can follow only one pattern which is very thoroughly ingrained in you, then you have closed the doors to all of that which is expressional.

What you are capable of is so marvelous that it is almost impossible to imagine what you could do if you achieved it. Don't say you can never get there. Get as far as you can with a full heart and with full conviction, then try to drive on a little further. To achieve something takes strength. You are not born with that strength, you have to gain it. Don't look at your exercises as something to make your muscles hurt, but as something that will help you to improve yourself. Know that you are a human being, that you are able to take life as it is. Life is not an escape. It is not an excuse. It is not idle cowardness. You must think, "I can do more this year than I did last year because I have grown meanwhile." Don't dull yourself with copying something or someone, remember that sometimes you absorb much more through your pores than through your head.

You must be humble in relation to your steady progress. Be thankful for what you have but recognize that you haven't gotten it all. We are all but a small part of what remains to be discovered, to be found out. Those who have attained even a great deal know that there still lie out there somewhere a thousand things yet to be discovered. You will find out that one life is not enough. You will want to have several lives in which to discover what there is to be discovered.

The right way of developing is to go at a steady pace and to get the most out of every situation. When you have reached a platform, look for the stairs leading up to the next platform. But be patient, don't want success too fast. Learn to wait. The platform on which you stand must not be an illusion. Above all, it must be deserved. It is impossible to remain for very long on a high platform if you don't have an absolute knowledge of what you

are doing. Operate within your own ability. Do not try to con-
quer things which are too far above you. They may kill you.
Sooner or later it will show that you have no base, that you
are just a hollow front. Audiences are very cruel with hollow
fronts. They will say, "Show me!," and if you don't show them
they will let you fall flat two miles down to your death. Go the
straight, direct way, don't skip anything. Never think that you
are better than anyone else. It is the nature of our existence on
this earth that no one is better than anyone else.

At the end of the forties when George Balanchine
moved with his company into the City Center, we
had long meetings together, and I favored the
idea of making a corps of ballet dancers and a
corps of modern dancers. There were many talented people in and around New York City, and I
wanted to bring them together to form a company
for which various choreographers of the modern
dance would come in and choreograph with the
pool of chosen dancers. The ballet accomplished
this but the modern dance did not. The various
choreographers would not let go of the members
of their companies. This kind of isolationism
among modern dance choreographers has caused
the audiences to take sides, and thereby modern
dance has failed to achieve recognition as a unit.
It was planned to include all styles of choreography in the company — so this was not their reason for holding back. The problem was that their
ego would not allow them to let go of the group
of dancers they had clustered around themselves.
About fifteen years later the same attempt was
made, the same people came together and wanted
to pool a group of dancers, but they could not get
the necessary financial backing. No one was willing to take the risk. Modern dance had done too

thorough a job of scattering itself in a thousand different directions.

You can do a lot with very little if you only know how. If you have something of value, if you have a plan, if you know what you are undertaking, if you have the intelligence to do it, you can accomplish it with very little help. If you can prove that you *have* something, the help will come.

> If you haven't the knowledge to implement a modern dance program, teach folk dance. Folk dance has form, organization, step patterns, relationships, and continuity. It is wrong to try to abstract when you don't even know what the word means. I constantly see abstractions of themes that are nothing more than miserably performed, dull conceptions of what the theme means. Do the forms that can be done at your level. An Irish jig takes great skill. A Yugoslavian folk dance is very difficult to accomplish. These are good forms which you can do if you lack the knowledge of making up your own. One should not look down on the forms established in folk dancing. Folk dancing is a highly developed skill. Skilled folk dancers have the feeling for rhythm and understand the responsibility one has to a beat and a pulse. You should see them do sword dances, you should watch the position of their feet. They are beautiful. If you can accomplish all of this, you are well on your way to becoming a good modern dancer.

I will never forget the great experience I had in the Cathedral in Strasbourg. It was dark inside the Cathedral so that you could not see clear to the top. It had the effect of funneling your whole attention upward. Light was coming through a beautifully painted window and caused a stream of reflection which

hit an altar with a crucifixion scene. It had the most unbeliev-
able effect of arresting your step, of making you stand still, of
giving you a heightened sense of being. How many times does
this happen? I have been in St. Peter's in Rome and in all of
the major cathedrals in Europe but none struck me with that
kind of meaningful space. There was a tension inside that
church which created the constant feeling of being uplifted.

> Your dances must be built from something within
> your self. It does not have to be concrete. It may
> be a very intangible thing. It may have a very
> wonderful, ethereal reason. You cannot do a
> dance and then decide what it is. Form has to
> come out of that to which it is related. That which
> causes the behavior determines the form.

If a decoration is placed on a basic structure without feeling for
the structure, it will be destructive. Decoration should be used
only if it serves to enhance the form and brings out more than
the basic naked form can do by itself. Some forms need a diversified statement. Others do not because they are self-sufficient.
You must train your senses, taste, and judgment. Training
means experience. Judgment is not learning what is black and
white.

> Life cannot be superimposed upon a piece of art.
> If it doesn't have it, it will never have it. The mes-
> sage of life must be given a work at birth. It is the
> same with us. If we do not have it, we will never
> have it. We cannot learn it out of a book, it must
> be learned by experience. It comes with the fine
> things like the fragrance of a rose.

Art is projected through the clarity of its form. It is the sum
total of something. Something spiritual comes across which is
not broadcast through the deed itself, but is manifested in the
manner in which you did it. The "how" in which you do it is
extremely important. It requires discipline.

Form is the shape of a content. Form without content becomes form for the sake of form. Inspiration has to be there to make a form live. The form should contain the original impetus out of which it was created. If the form emerged from an emotional ingredient, then that emotional ingredient must be there.

You should not dance academically. It has no departure, no breath, no life. The academician moves within a group of rules. Two plus two are four. The artist learns rules so that he can break them. Two plus two are five. Both are right from a different point of view.

> An example: a rule is that your knee has to be over your toe when you perform a plie. Sometimes you have to turn the knee in and break the rule. If you know the rule and technique, then you can bring that knee in without getting hurt. For some things the knee must be in order for the shape and form to be right according to that which you are communicating. Another rule is that when walking you transfer the weight from straight knee to straight knee with an adjustment of the general velocity. You may want to walk in an awkward way with hanging knees for the reason of getting an idea across. You have broken the rule of walking right, but you have entered a form through which you could communicate. Yet if you don't know the rules you won't know how to break them. You might make the baggy knees the norm and the shuffling forward the rule. If you don't know the rules you won't know what to go away from, and there are millions of departures. Your form will often demand that you break rules.

There are a thousand points of view. Hindemith and I were at the same conservatory in Frankfort. We both received the same kind of basic training. Then he departed in the way of finding out how music could be made. He used combinations of many different kinds, the twelve-tone scale, the cacophony, the dissonances, broad chords requiring more than ten fingers. He became absorbed in tone qualities and the tone relationships of intervals, but before he died he came back to the classic style. You can work, for example, with just the hands and arms and develop them to the nth degree until they are marvelous — but you will come to a dead end where it will be necessary to return to the body in order to incorporate your findings into the body as such in order to go on moving.

There are books written about circles and squares. The ancient people understood them. You will find them amongst the old Egyptian ruins. Some of the old Mayan ruins were temples with a circle or a square of stone tops which were of great significance. No one originated these forms. They have always existed. One day while walking about Rome I came about a church called St. Clement. There was an entrance at one of its sides leading downstairs. Two flights below the church was an ancient heathen worship ground. After passing several hallways which were very low, I came to a chamber with seats around the outside. In the center was a square altar. The old mystical signs were still visible everywhere in the room. They had been hammered into the stone. The worshipers had worn away the earth where they had been sitting. On top of this chamber was a very common assembly hall and on top of that was the church. The more intelligent the ancient peoples were, the more mystical was the form in its use and significance. There is more to a round than just making a circle. You will have to run in circles for many days before you will know what a circle is. Then all of a sudden you will realize that you are not yourself anymore, that your space is dynamic and powerful and that you have to master that force. Turning is almost a dervish exercise with the world suddenly going around and you feeling very calm and quiet. If you work for half a year on circles, your turns will become different.

Style requires a certain form, and you have to stick to that form. You have to discipline yourself to it, or you will not get a good theater piece. The characteristic has to be maintained in every aspect of the work. Even a walk has to be practiced. There are a thousand walks. If you don't know which walk to do, you will just wobble and walk as best you can, but nothing will be created by it. A walk without a characteristic is as good as non-existent, it is pitiful. It would be better to lower the curtain and go home.

The line between emoting and emotion is different with each person. You have to discover within yourself when your technique arrives at a point where your movement becomes an experience as such. You must master the physical experience so that it becomes a kinesthetic experience. You will discover through this kinesthetic experience that a relationship is established within the body which coordinates the flow of movement and the flow of animation. You will find out that movement can contain only a certain amount of emotion before the emotion outdoes the physical experience. When this overtaxation happens, you have overdrawn. Emotion is a stimulus, not an end result. It is arrived at but not emphasized. Emotion is the stimulus which gives the movement its coloring, its reason for being. Since the emotion is the stimulus for the movement, it is, therefore, both the stimulus and a part of the end result.

The face is of course the mirror of all that goes on, but it should not be more prominent than is intended and it should not substitute for all that which isn't going on in the body. Facial muscles are very small and very sensitive. If the face does too much it turns into mugging. The face becomes a thing in itself. It overdoes things because the body doesn't understand what to do and therefore the face substitutes. The face should have a relationship to the whole attitude. It should enliven the attitude and complement it. A dancer's face is not a mask. I sometimes look at the eyes instead of looking at the movement and I very often see absolutely dead eyes inside a multiple-moving body.

> Your body is your language. Cultivate your language. Be able to say what you want. If you are supposed to be in second position with your bottom sticking out, then it is right according to the form. If your bottom is not supposed to be sticking out and it is, it is an insult to the form. The form is changed from a form into nothing. A form is a silent thing which has achieved a shape. The shape will be as exciting as that which you put into it. It will be clear only as you give it clarity. It can have only the shape which you give it. It can achieve life only because you have given it such. The responsibility is yours.

Check yourself and see if you are willing to sacrifice yourself for something that is bigger than you are. You must know to what you have put your mind. If you are in dance just to satisfy your ego, then be a nice admirer but get out of the field. If you are dabbling in dance just for your own satisfaction, go right ahead, but don't pass on your half-knowledges to people who are searching. Dance is the noblest art there is. Sacrifice is necessary, even if that sacrifice is your ego. This does not mean that you should become a limp rag and let everyone wipe his dirty feet on you. Your inner self must give you hope, strength, belief, a power of dedication without resorting to the ugly thing of cheating. Make-believes are not worth anything; they have their own doom written within themselves; they only wait for you to find out, and by the time you do find out you will have wasted years and years and years. Waste you must, but waste in the right direction.

> The inner man is a fine little point where your being comes together. If you could externalize it, it would not be bigger than the head of a pin. In size of volume it is not a fraction of a fraction of an atom. This inner man is like the center of a hurricane. The secret of a hurricane is its eye. The eye is calm. If you destroy that eye you destroy the hurricane. If you can't be as calm as the eye of the hurricane which holds all the answers to the devastating storm of the outside, you can't hold yourself up in the world of dilemma and battle. There is no force that does not come from an utter calm. Sensitivity, the power to absorb and to register, is the calm of the eye which starts that outer passion and tremor.

When you have discovered that inner self, you can call yourself a dancer, but don't get snooty about it. Dancers don't live in ivory towers. If you put that inner man on a scale, it wouldn't weigh more than a hundredth of an ounce. The more you know, the humbler you become, if you really know it. This is growing, studying, living. Dance is life. Know that you are alive.

BY WAY OF CONCLUSION

We all make mistakes. There are no saints, and if you find one he probably is a bore. Personality has color, and there is no personality without a focus.

— HANYA HOLM

A Vignette of Her Personality

HANYA, blue-eyed and blond, stands five feet two inches tall and weighs about 110 pounds. With a birdlike expression she seems to look around questioningly and somehow warily, eager to absorb but also ready to react at a moment's notice. And yet she quietly radiates the security of tremendous energies, wisely spent, of a driving force which has carved out an inevitable path.

When some people stand in the limelight, it is easy to take veil after veil from their official face. Not so with Hanya. She seems very human and accessible, and yet there is something about her which is almost impenetrable. The silver spoon with which she was born was an iron will and self-discipline. She carries around a built-in philosophy which gives her the strength not to be fooled by life nor to fool herself. She knows how much to take because she knows how much she is willing to do herself. She is a cool fanatic with a heightened sensitivity and receptivity to experience, an ability to absorb and to teach what she has absorbed and experienced. She is that strange creature who is half artist, half teacher, and who is both in a measured manner as well as with a burning fever and fervor. She can stand with both feet on the ground while her mind is on a most beautiful flight into nowhere or into the impossible, from where it may bring back to reality a rare image or a new idea.

The artistic achievement of a person should be considered ideally as an independent phenomenon, independent from the mental make-up of the person. Although we know that the psyche of the artist conditions and often directs the artistic output, we, the public, must not equate personality and artistry when considering the latter. Nor must we be influenced by the biographer, whose task it is to bring into focus everything that has any bearing on the artist's growth, the sociocultural background as much as psychological factors.

Hanya Holm, the artist, may be valued differently by different people — as every artist is — but her record as a contributor to the international dance scene speaks for itself, some incontestable facts that have become history cannot be misread. As a stranger to the New World, she was fortunate in arriving at a time when, in the thirties, the American modern dance unfolded its potentialities as a new and vital force; when the colleges in the States began to embrace the modern dance as a tool for educational purposes; when, in the forties, the American musical became mature and developed into a very distinct and indigenous art form. In all three spheres Hanya's contribution was far-reaching and of lasting value. Most important of all, particularly for the generation of young dancers in the fifties and sixties, has been Hanya's approach to technique based on her philosophy of setting the dancer free and giving him the tools with which to develop his individual creative ability. At a time when the stress in the modern dance was on the dancer's psychodramatic experience, Hanya kept away from it and taught, above all, the kinetic experience, the logic and understanding of movement per se.

In the recital field her work, spanning only the years from 1936 to 1944, proved her lyric talent as much as the weighty dramatic statement, playful and humorous notions as much as large theatrical and architectural forms. Her work in the lyric theater, from 1948 to this day, is connected with the climactic achievements in this area, be it Kiss Me, Kate, The Golden Apple, or My Fair Lady. Although it cannot easily be spelled out in black and white, her direct and indirect effect as dance educator has been immeasurable.

In some respects, the artist and the person are inseparable

in their impact on their environment. As educator, the dancer and technician in her can hardly be separated from Hanya the philosopher. Here the image of the entire personality came into play. It also made itself felt in her need to experiment as artist and teacher, a fact that led to so many "firsts" in her career. Having been often ahead of her time has been the logical consequence of her inquisitive nature, of probing the reasons for all *whys,* and of believing firmly in herself. Her life and success as dancer-choreographer-teacher may not have been glamorous but it has been solid, it may have lacked the sparkle of the headline personality but it has become an influential and viable image in the life of many dancers and students who search for their identity.

Every person's life is colored by the way he sees the world, but he is also the person the world sees in him. The result is a multicolored mosaic. Hanya has had a long career not only as a performing and creative artist and as a teacher — but also as a human being. It often seems as if she had practiced to develop the great understanding she has for each student and each friend. Most of the people who have come close to her sense "the great effort and sacrifice that lie behind her and that made her arrive where she is today," as one of them put it. This student realized that her drive to succeed in her career must be closely related to failures in her personal life, failures which instilled in her such high and rigid standards and make her often appear as a taskmaster. Or a testimony in a similar vein: "I know she has great warmth, but her past has not allowed her to show much of it." Or: "I'm not sure she is a warm person, though I wish to think so. But she is a total personality and gives you the feeling that she has the capacity of living consciously each new day. She is inspiring."

Walter Terry says about her: "I have known Hanya for thirty years without becoming a close friend of hers. I find her an extremely gentle woman, though she has an enormous determination, and her career attests to this. She is soft-spoken, has a very winsome smile and a marvelous sense of humor. She is very articulate, as a matter of fact, so articulate that sometimes in class she gives a lecture. She needs to, there is a compulsion to speak about something she has just discovered or something that was renewed in her. She is never at a loss for words. But she is just as good a listener as she is a chatterer. There is a very stubborn side to her, but I have never seen her angry or impatient. In all the classes I have seen — and I have taken classes with her — there is determination and discipline but never fury. I know she has faults but I just don't happen to know what they are. She is a very good mother and a proud grandmother."

Hanya would be the last person to claim that she is without faults. She is constantly trying to find out who Hanya Holm really is. "You don't recognize your voice," she says. "Sometimes I feel I am too close to myself. Then I wish I could be someone else and meet myself." Or on another occasion: "I often ask myself: Who are you? I talk and don't know who is speaking. I can talk to myself as if I were someone else."

She would find it ridiculous to pretend that she does not believe in the importance of herself. But she sees man as a vessel with the purpose of serving a purpose. From this, if from no other viewpoint, her *leit-motif* is an altruistic, not a selfish one. "I need a solid basis from which I can swing freely. But freedom is not a license, it is utter discipline."

Hanya knows about impatience as does everyone else. But she would not permit it to rule her feelings and actions. She has always held that you must give yourself time for any creative work, that you must be able to wait until ideas mature and fall as ripe fruits into the artist's lap. She has learned that this notion of time is an essential prerequisite for the creative process. It has become clear to her that patience with time (to watch ideas grow on you) and impatience with oneself (during work no one could be less self-indulgent and more exacting than Hanya) are fundamental to any artistic accomplishment. When, shortly after her arrival in America in 1931, Sol Hurok told her: "I give you one year to form a company, and then I'll send you on tour!" Hanya replied: "No, thank you, it will take me five years, and I know you can't wait that long." It took her almost six years.

But she also knows that there is nothing static about her. She can easily change her point of view without giving up certain principles, in life as much as in her work. She avoids visualizing preconceived ideas or any definite goal. "I just go and try to do my best. I *live* the way things happen around me. To live *it*, to live each thing is essential." Hanya admits to being able to adjust immediately to anything, but this then creates a feeling of utter loneliness or lostness in her.

Most of the time she reacts instinctively. "When I have to reason things out they disappear." On the other hand, she will take nothing for granted and must find out the reason for everything that exists. Again, "If something hits me as a totality of being, then I don't search for any reason, then I know it is something real I can hold onto. I am looking for the totality of things, I cannot separate or compartmentalize. A rose is a part of the mystery of creation to me: its color, form, fragrance, they are one and the same."

Hanya may appear as a very realistic person, and in many ways she is. But in all her major decisions she relies on her instincts and follows them blindly. In Dresden when the question came up of whether Hanya or Mary Wigman's sister should be sent to America, her reactions were immediate: "Intuitively I said I'll do it, I'll go. I had a feeling that something was wrong with Germany, that drastic changes were in store, but I also had an inexplicable sensation that this was the thing for me to do."

Whether Hanya can hear the grass grow and whether she has some extrasensory perception is difficult to say. But she feels that "there is nothing cemented in me, my senses come first, long before my mind begins to work. This instinctive reaction to things and people often means that I shy away from people, that I quickly build up a protective barrier against my instincts rather than against the people. As if I were afraid to be hurt. But this of course people do not know and would not understand if they did know."

Basically, Hanya has always been a shy person. She has never had a flair for socializing and she could never set out purposely to ingratiate herself with influential and powerful people. But, from time to time, such an ability may be of great advantage for the leader of a dance company. It became crucial in the early forties when the very existence of her company was at stake. Hanya received a few thousand dollars from friends in those critical days. This help, however, was insufficient. The financial needs for mounting new dance creations and keeping the dancers together could no longer be met. Within a few years the demands of the public had changed too. In the thirties, simple costumes, which the company sewed and dyed, sufficed; a pianist, who could also play the cello and accordion, accompanied them. In the forties, the audience expected an orchestra and far more glamorous costumes. "Unfortunately," Hanya says, "I did not have enough or the right social connections. It was my fault. I have never cared too much for kowtowing. So I did not know where to get the money from and had to dissolve the company."

Hanya's studios have always been a world very characteristic of Hanya. When she arrived in New York, the Mary Wigman School started in Steinway Hall on Manhattan's 57th Street. In 1936 she moved into her own studio at 215 West 11th Street in Greenwich Village. This studio is fondly remembered by everyone who worked there. It was a large two-story room of great charm, opening on a patio. The fine floor measured 40 by 45 feet. At one end, under the balcony which housed the office and faculty room, there was a large and unusual collection of percussion instruments. The rest of the first two floors of the building was occupied by dressing rooms and shower rooms.

Strict rules were observed. The mornings were reserved for

the work of the company, the afternoons were devoted to three professional classes, the evenings were given over to special courses and men's classes. On Saturdays Hanya gave classes for laymen and children, and during holiday periods there were concentrated courses for dancers, teachers, and students.

Hanya had to give up this studio in 1947, at a time when she was certain that she would not form another company of her own. From then on she gave her classes at Michael's Studio on Eighth Avenue, and she moved from there to the Dance Players' Studios on Sixth Avenue in 1959. When these studios had to close in the winter of 1967 to make room for a new building going up on the site, Hanya gave up the idea of running a studio altogether. A great era had finally come to an end. There is no longer any Hanya Holm School of the Dance in New York City.

"Hanya's drive and tenacity have always been dominant factors in her life," Louise Kloepper says. "She was a very disciplined person, worked hard at whatever task she set for herself. She was limited movementwise because of knee injuries sustained early in her dancing career. This did not deter her in any way. . . . She was always very good to me and even through the Depression years which were rough on all of us in many ways, Hanya and I had a fine relationship. I will always be indebted to her for all I was able to learn in working with her."

"My most vivid memory of Hanya is the very first day that I met her," Valerie Bettis says. "I had been running from studio to studio to see where I would end up . . . a 'serious' young lady from Texas, bound and determined to be a dancer.

"I spoke to the secretary outside the studio on West 11th Street and was probably overheard by Hanya, who invited me to come in and speak with her. We were in the balcony which overlooked the studio, from below I could hear the sounds of drums . . . and in front of me was Hanya with the long blond hair streaming down her back, the bright blue eyes viewing me with their usual straightforward look, with always the hint of laughter coming just round the corner. I only remember one question and my answer.

Hanya: And *why* do you want to dance?
Me: I want to be the greatest dancer in the world!
Pause
Hanya (holding back laughter): That will take some time, my dear.

"And so I enrolled. I was fortunate enough that very fall to be a part of the augmented group in *Trend*. That meant rehearsing from nine to twelve in the morning, classes from one to six, and rehearsing in the evening from eight to twelve. Because of the complexity and size of the work we rehearsed in a huge loft somewhere, and I can still see Hanya perched on top of a high ladder with, I believe, a megaphone in her hand . . . 'Straighten your leg!' . . . Me: 'It *is* straight!' Of course, she was right, and I was just a smarty. I performed and worked with Hanya for three years, during which time I worked so hard, what remains is a blur of our tours, and classes, classes, classes.

"I consider myself extremely lucky to have had the opportunity to work with her and her staff at that time . . . this was no 'stylistic technique,' but strong theory, solid training of the body, and an equal emphasis on creativity. This basis is still what I teach and move from. Even when I left, Hanya — she was marvelous in her concern for my future — arranged for my first teaching job at Perry-Mansfield, which was a wonderful opportunity for me . . . and was ever present at my debut concert, and all those thereafter. We have a warm personal friendship which I cherish."

" I have great respect for Hanya," says another dancer who was in Hanya's company between 1936 and 1940. "She is a brilliant woman, and because she is so clever she is well aware of her limitations too. I learned a great deal from her and make use of it in my teaching, particularly when it comes to the creative development of a subject matter through participation of the students. She gave us all very much, but, at least at that time, I think Hanya needed in return the emotional loyalty of her group members very badly, and not everyone was willing to pay the price of utter dedication."

For quite some time Glen Tetley did. "Hanya was my first dance teacher," he tells me, "and her influence on my career was most important. I came late to dancing as a medical student. She impressed me through the organic way of her teaching, her meaningful, metaphysical approach through which she made many things clear to me and removed the many misgivings I then had. I was on a scholarship and lived in the house where she had her studio on 11th Street. This gave me an opportunity to be around her for ten to twelve hours a day. She almost gave me the feeling of an Indian teacher because, as with a guru, I found her way of life a beautiful unity and she understood how to give me a purpose in life. Yes, there was something Eastern about her, also in her untroubled fluidity of moving. She was a rich mine of information for me. We were close enough so that I could absorb some of her supreme idealism.

"After two years of apprenticeship I began to teach for her. I still remember that I asked her before my first class what I should prepare. 'Don't prepare anything,' she said. 'Open yourself to them, give what they need and what you can give.' There was magic in her teaching, though. Where other teachers stop, at the physicality level, she began, and presented her architecture of the dance, an awareness of space and gravity, a close analysis of music.

"She has the most beautiful mind in dance. As far as she herself is concerned, she has too much self-criticism and is unable to accept anything second best. I suspect that she can't totally release emotion. There is enormous strength in her, a concealed steel strength. Perhaps she may not be above cruelty but then only to create a feeling of strength in you. As a teacher, she can give herself fully and develop for you a strong basis from which you can go in your own direction."

Loyalty is one emotional statement in life to which she

clings. She has been loyal to Mary Wigman through the years. It is her strong belief in a true teacher-pupil relationship that has given deeper meaning to her own life and her feelings for Mary Wigman. One can often hear Hanya say that we must not lose sight of where we started our career. It is almost a parental and protective feeling which she herself has so often developed toward her pupils, and nothing can hurt her more easily or more deeply than an indication of her students not showing a sign of gratitude toward her.

She can take criticism as much as she can be hard on other people. She has a sternness and devotion to principles and standards not always easy to live up to. She can sympathize with failure, with not quite making it, with personal troubles and emotional difficulties, but not with self-pity and smugness, with laziness and unpunctuality or, above all, with phoniness. Her greatest irritations have always been "the empty people," those "who find security in something they don't own," as she says. "They are the imitators, the easy-getters who want it all in a nutshell." Then she can be merciless in bearing down on and rejecting a person.

One of her disciples remembers how Hanya can take criticism, however direct or indirect it may be. This person recalls the days in the early forties when almost the entire company had left Hanya and when she was facing two students in her class. "What shall we do?" the former student remembers Hanya saying. "What can we do but go on?" And she gave one of her wonderful classes for two as if there had been twenty. "Hanya would accept criticism from wherever it came, but never defeat," her student says. "Hanya is a most complex human being. Those with a very strongly built, stable ego could get the most out of working with her. But like most people who grew very strong and fortified within through their own crushing life experiences, Hanya's reactions were often hard to take by those whose ways were not set and who could not take punishment or verbal lashing so easily, however well it may have been meant. Particularly in helping build a personality through class work or in the creative field, a less secure person could be destroyed."

A student who finally did not choose to make the dance her career explains her experience with Hanya: "When you have studied with her you know yourself a little better, you know what your capacities are, you can measure yourself, and Hanya is very much interested in getting you to this point. She gave me more self-confidence, the possibility of coping better with problems in other fields. I was able to understand my emotions a little better, to have a leash on myself. She was pleased to hear this and said that this was one of the things she hoped would emerge from her dance classes. She does not want to make dancers only, but wants to give you a feeling for yourself in the world. She makes of you a person who is not afraid of herself, she makes you aware of the fact that there are no limits to making things possible."

"It is true, because she is such a hard taskmaster she has destroyed some people who cannot stand up to what she demands," Don Redlich says. "She demands a great deal from everyone, but some people take this as a personal affront to them, saying to themselves, 'She doesn't like me,' or 'Why is she picking on me all the time.' I think if she picks on you you are very lucky, then she is interested in you and she sees something that she wishes to correct or make you find."

Hanya once told Mr. Redlich, "If you stand in front of a mountain, don't try to go around it, dig through it, do everything you can to get to the other end by experiencing it the hard way. It may cost you some energy, but it is worth it."

"I never knew that I was funny," Don Redlich continues, "until Hanya found it out and gave me very specific problems in the area of humor. In other words, Hanya influenced me in finding myself, in digging into myself and discovering for myself my own way of expressing things. My personal relation ship to her developed from that of a student enthralled by his teacher. Then as I went on and worked with her professionally, I had many reactions of both love and hate, particularly hatred when I was hurt not to have been engaged by her to appear in one of her shows. But later I realized I shouldn't have taken it personally. She sticks to what she needs to get, and come hell and high water she is not prone to make any compromises. Whatever stands in her way stands in her way. If she has a concept she is going to hold to that, and everything has to fit. If you personally don't fit, too bad for you. Not that she is not a good friend, but I had to become independent and strong enough first not to lean on the teacher. It was a phase of development for me during which she remained steadfast and continued to show her interest and concern. There was great endurance on her part. But I could never quite figure her out. There seems to be a dichotomy in her personality. I could only be aware of it and respond to her honestly and openly. I suppose that is the way she wants it."

When criticism, even if sharp or biting, can kill an artist or would-be artist, then we should agree with Carlyle, who thought that in such a case the sooner he is despatched the better. To a teacher, however, psychology is of the essence. Hanya may be irritated by a class and its failure, and let loose one of her tongue-lashing speeches which often may take up the rest of the session. Again, while some students reported they learned their lesson and gained by it, others were bewildered and hurt. On the other hand, Hanya knows how to feel her way through a class, to measure its pulse beat.

Juana de Laban finds that Hanya can be a very good friend, but not in the usual sense, "because for such friendships Hanya has not enough time. If she gives her time she expects you to benefit from it. She would scrutinize your ideas which you bring to her, she would search for your purposes and intents whether you are fully aware of what you are planning to do, and she is continually interested in helping you on your way. Sometimes she can be rather rough on you in relation to what your own goals and discoveries are, but even then she remains interested in your artistic quality, and if a person is able to respond to that, then she feels gratified."

Miss de Laban thinks that it is also very difficult to be

accepted as a colleague by Hanya. "You have to find a way to be accepted, and again, as on the level of friendship, she does not allow you to feel like a colleague of hers until she realizes that you too have found your own way, your own approach to your work. If she senses that that is happening, then she is perfectly willing to offer you a possibility either to work with her or to recommend you for a job."

"Her contribution to my own personal vitality was great," Alwin Nikolais says. "Later on it was even more important than in Bennington between 1938 and 1939 when I first worked with Hanya. I studied with her at that time as well as with Martha, Doris, and Charles — all conveyed to me the foundation of the American dance scene. Being with them gave me a feeling of being part of the history of what to my mind later will be indicated as one of the most vital periods in the United States. The mind of the critics in the thirties and forties was focused on the expressional creations. Therefore, when expressional poeticism was not the forte of an individual, he or she might easily have gotten lost in the critical reviews of the time. This is bound to happen. . . . Hanya's legacy to us can be continued as in what I am doing in the Playhouse, for instance, however much I may have extended her theories and techniques. . . . I remember once Hanya angrily remarking, in a class where dancers seemed to have been in a state of stupidity, after a few curse words in German: 'Dancers in the head do not have to have straw!' One of her big premises was that dancers, although required to use their intuition, also have to be equipped with fine intelligence, that poaching around on the edges was not sufficient. If one knows Hanya, one knows her brilliant mind and the great intelligence that is there as well as the deep insight into esthetic matters."

Broad in her interests in regard to her craft, Hanya has never believed in limiting her personal activities to specialized areas either. In her concert days, she dyed her own costumes, arranged the lighting, played the piano. Earlier, when she had still more time, she enjoyed painting and woodcarving. In her New York apartment she has grown plants and has kept tropical fish, dogs, and cats as well as birds. She plays chess, is an animated worker of crossword puzzles and an excellent cook with a discriminating palate, particularly for the German cuisine to which she is still partial; she is an ardent reader of good books, a conscientious letter writer, and a pleasant raconteur. She knows a lot about lace-making, embroidery, and flowers. She can talk philosophy as well as high fidelity. She has preserved her love for conversation, an art almost lost in our overstimulated, hectic world in which the mass media are about to silence our thoughts.

There are many hundreds of people she has met, taught, and worked with who have always thought of Hanya as a friend: from the distinguished theologian Paul Tillich to her former factotum Thelma Cowan; from the famous actors who come to her classes to the little girls who want to become second Hanyas. And probably her most devoted friend is Klaus Holm, her son, for whom, in the midst of all bustling and hustling, she has always had time.

Characteristic too of Hanya's personality is the help and encouragement she has often given to embryonic dance groups and mushrooming associations. But she has never given her name as a mere token. If she gives it, she always insists that it must mean something. So she has attended meetings and talks, carefully studied plans and declarations, and made thoughtful suggestions when she believed she could be helpful. Was it a generous waste of time? Hardly, since it helped to keep her abreast of current trends and thoughts throughout the country.

However logically and fluently she verbalizes her thoughts in English, her word pattern will apparently always have a Germanic flavor. Her descriptive faculty is precise, beautifully lucid, but on occasion it produces astounding figures of speech. After a talk of hers at the University of Denver in 1936 a columnist wrote: "She does use odd combinations of words which make listening to her a delight." There are hundreds of these Hanyaisms fondly remembered by her friends and students. The repertoire is almost endless: "Keep the beat, but undermine it." "Use the foot as if you would pick up a flower with your toes." "Make your head a fifth carriage and not the meeting place of the intelligentsia." One day she explained syncopation as "an undone pulse"; and trying to impress her theory class that skill is not acquired all at once, she said: "What we have doesn't always come in wallops. It comes not always in knockouts." Admonishing her class to achieve a heightened sense of perception, she repeatedly says: "Feel it, children, don't schlop it."

Along with the involuntary humor inherent in these phrases, there is an intensity which reveals the originality with which Hanya reaches out to communicate and to make herself understood. And she succeeds.

Whatever her speech pattern may be, she never thinks of herself as having become an "American," although she acclimatized and adjusted herself to her new environment very easily and quickly. But she is too thorough and methodical a person to pretend to be American. While she realizes that her grandchildren are true Americans, she likes to think of herself as an international artist and teacher whose roots were in Europe but whose headquarters are in America. For no one who comes to the New World at a mature age can the transformation become complete. On one level, on certain edges the European will be noticeable. If assimilation were only a matter of adjustment to all surface appearances, it would not be difficult. But through her way of thinking alone she is reminded that her mind is still in Europe though her heart is here. Or is it on certain occasions the other way round? "I know I think in English," she says, "but the way I say things often sounds German." Or doesn't she think in German, and her thoughts have an English sound?

But, in the last analysis, it is not our speech pattern that decides for us where we belong, but our feelings. She had made up her mind about her feelings as far back as 1932. Hanya knows that one day God will not ask her whether she felt more American or European, but how many fine dances and dancers did she make. The answer cannot be too difficult. It is recorded in dance history.

Chronology

IN GERMANY:

Euripedes' Bacchae

Dramatization of Plato's Farewell to His Friends
   Open-air Theater in Ommen, Holland Summer 1928 and
   1929

Choreographed and danced the role of the Princess in Igor
   Stravinsky's L'Histoire du Soldat, Schauspielhaus, Dresden, 1929

Das Totenmal (based on a poem and score by Albert Talhoff)
   Associate director and co-dancer with Mary Wigman, Munich, 1930

IN AMERICA:

Choreography for Concert Dances
   First Program presented at Broadway Theatre, Denver, November 1936:
   1. Salutation
   2. Drive
   3. Dance in Two Parts
   4. Sarabande
   5. In Quiet Space
   6. City Nocturne
   7. Four Chromatic Eccentricities
   8. Primitive Rhythm
   9. Festive Rhythm
   Trend
      Bennington Festival, August 1937
      Mecca Temple (New York City Center), December 1937
   Etudes
   Dance of Introduction
      Y.M.H.A., New York, April 1938

Dance Sonata
Dance of Work and Play
Metropolitan Daily
    Bennington Festival, August 1938
    Guild Theatre, New York, February 1939
Tragic Exodus
    Guild Theatre, New York, February 1939
They Too Are Exiles
    On transcontinental tour, 1939
    Adelphi Theatre, New York, January 1940
The Golden Fleece
    Mansfield Theatre, New York, March 1941
From This Earth
    Fine Arts Center Theatre, Colorado Springs, Colorado, August 1941
What So Proudly We Hail
Namesake
    Fine Arts Center Theatre, Colorado Springs, August 1942
Parable
Suite of Four Dances
    Central High School of Needle Trades, New York, January 1943
Orestes and the Furies
    Fine Arts Center Theatre, Colorado Springs, August 1943
What Dreams May Come
    Fine Arts Center Theatre, Colorado Springs, August 1944
Walt Whitman Suite
The Gardens of Eden
    Fine Arts Center Theatre, Colorado Springs, August 1945
Dance for Four
Windows
    Fine Arts Center Theatre, Colorado Springs, August 1946
And So Ad Infinitum (The Insect Comedy)
    Fine Arts Center Theatre, Colorado Springs, August 1947
Xochipili
    Fine Arts Center Theatre, Colorado Springs, August 1948
History of a Soldier
Ionization
    Fine Arts Center Theatre, Colorado Springs, August 1949
Five Old French Dances
    Fine Arts Center Theatre, Colorado Springs, August 1950
Prelude

Quiet City
 Fine Arts Center Theatre, Colorado Springs, August 1951
Kindertotenlieder
Concertino da Camera
 Fine Arts Center Theatre, Colorado Springs, August 1952
Ritual
Temperament and Behavior
 Fine Arts Center Theatre, Colorado Springs, August 1953
Prelude I and II
Presages
 Fine Arts Center Theatre, Colorado Springs, August 1954
L'Histoire du Soldat
 Wheeler Opera House, Aspen (Colorado) Festival, August
  1954
Desert Drone
Pavane (from Menotti's St. Sebastian Ballet)
Sousa March
 Perkins Hall Auditorium, Colorado Springs, August 1955
Preludio and Loure (Bach's Partita No. 3)
 Fine Arts Center Theatre, Colorado Springs, August 1956
Ozark Suite
 Brooklyn Institute of Arts and Sciences, December 1957
Chanson Triste
You Can't Go Home Again
Ozark Suite
 Fine Arts Center Theatre, Colorado Springs, August 1957
Music for an Imaginary Ballet
 Broadmoor International Theatre, Colorado Springs, Au-
  gust 1961
Figure of Predestination
Toward the Unknown Region
 Fine Arts Center Theatre, Colorado Springs, August 1963
Theatrics
 Fine Arts Center Theatre, Colorado Springs, August 1964
Spooks
 Armstrong Hall, Colorado Springs, August 1967

Choreography for Musicals
 The Eccentricities of Davey Crockett (from Ballet Ballads;
  choreography and direction) Maxine Elliott's Theatre, May
  1948
 The Insect Comedy (choreography, direction in collaboration
  with José Ferrer) New York City Center, June 1948

Kiss Me, Kate
  Century Theatre, December 1948
  Coliseum, London, March 1951
The Liar
  Broadhurst Theatre, May 1950
Out of This World
  Century Theatre, December 1950
My Darlin' Aida
  Winter Garden Theatre, October 1952
The Golden Apple
  The Phoenix Theatre, March 1954
Reuben, Reuben
  (tryout) Shubert Theatre, Boston, October 1955
My Fair Lady
  Mark Hellinger Theatre, March 1956
  Drury Lane Theatre, April 1958
  Habimah National Theatre, Tel Aviv, February 1964
Where's Charley?
  Opera House, Manchester, November 1957
  Palace Theatre, London, February 1958
Christine
  46th Street Theatre, April 1960
Camelot
  Majestic Theatre, December 1960
Anya
  Ziegfeld Theatre, November 1965

Choreography and Stage Direction for Operas
  The Ballad of Baby Doe
    Opera House, Central City, Colorado, July 1956
  Orpheus and Euridice
    Queen Elizabeth Theatre, Vancouver, B.C., July 1959
    O'Keefe Centre, Toronto, May 1962

Choreography for Non-Musical Plays
  $E=MC^2$
    Brander Matthews Hall, Columbia University, June 1948
  Blood Wedding
    New Stages, February 1949

Choreography for Movies
  The Vagabond King
    Paramount, September 1956

Choreography for Television
    Metropolitan Daily
        NBC (first modern dance production on TV; Hanya Holm
            Company), May 1939
    The Dance and the Drama
        "Folio" Program, Canadian Broadcasting Company, 1957
    Pinocchio
        NBC, October 1957
    Dinner with the President
        Televised from Washington (choreography for dance com-
            pany of six), 1963
    Several radio and television interviews

List of Essays

"The Dance, the Artist-Teacher, and the Child" in *Progressive Education*, 1935

"The German Dance in the American Scene" in *Modern Dance*, edited by Virginia Stewart, E. Weyhe, New York, 1935

"Mary Wigman"
in *Dance Observer*, November 1935

"Dance on the Campus — Athletics or Art?"
in *Dance Magazine*, February 1937

"*Trend* Grew Upon Me"
in *Magazine of Art*, March 1938

"The Mary Wigman I Know"
in *The Dance Has Many Faces*, edited by Walter Sorell, The World Publishing Company, 1951; new revised edition, Columbia University Press, 1966

List of Honors

New York Times Award for *Trend*, "best dance composition of the year" (John Martin, dance critic)

1937–1938

Dance Magazine Award for *Tragic Exodus*, "best group choreography in Modern Dance"

1938–1939

Hanya Holm represented "Women in Art" at the Centennial Celebration at Duke University

1939

New York Drama Critics' Award for the choreography of *Kiss Me, Kate*

1948–1949

Critics' Circle Citation for *The Golden Apple* "as the best musical of the season"

1954

Nomination for Tony Award for the choreography of *My Fair Lady*

1957

Award from the Federation of Jewish Philanthropies for "outstanding contribution to the Modern Dance Movement in America"

1959

Honorary degree of Doctor of Fine Arts from Colorado College, Colorado Springs

1960

Sources

Various statements by others than the author are included in this book. Those from printed sources are identified where they appear. Those attributed simply to an individual (not to a publication) are derived from interviews, tape recordings, or letters. The following are the source materials on which this work is based:

Hanya Holm: Interviews, tapes, class observations. Quotes from *The Dance Has Many Faces*, edited by Walter Sorell; *Modern Dance*, edited by Virginia Stewart; *Magazine of Art*, March 1938; *Progressive Education*, October 1935 ("The Dance, the Artist-Teacher, and the Child"); scrap books

Walter Sorell: "Hanya Holm: from Convent to 'My Fair Lady,'" *Dance Magazine*, January 1957; "The Totality in Hanya Holm's Work," *Impulse* 1958; *The Dance Has Many Faces* (quote from "The Actor and the Dance")

John Martin: *Introduction to the Dance; The Modern Dance; America Dancing*; reviews: *The New York Times*

Walter Terry: Interview on tape; reviews: *Boston Herald, New York Herald Tribune*

Margaret Lloyd: *The Borzoi Book of Modern Dance*; reviews in *The Christian Science Monitor.*

Alwin Nikolais: Tapes spoken on Hanya Holm

Dr. Juana de Laban: Tapes spoken on Hanya Holm

Don Redlich: Tape spoken on Hanya Holm; interviews

K. Wright Dunkley: Transcript of tape recordings taken during Hanya Holm's classes at Colorado College in 1964 (manuscript)

Arch Lauterer: "Arch Lauterer — Poet in the Theatre," *Impulse* 1959

Carolyn Durand Brooks: "Hanya Holm Gets a Dance Festival" in (*The Colorado College Magazine*, Fall 1965)

Jack Anderson: "Hanya Holm Asks and Answers," *Dance Magazine*, August 1965

Newspaper and magazine clippings: *Theatre Arts Monthly* (February 1937), *Variety, Colorado Springs Gazette Telegraph, Philadelphia Inquirer, New Haven Journal-Courier, The Free Press* (Colorado Springs), *Denver Post, The News Chronicle and Daily Dispatch* (Manchester), *Manchester Evening News, Daily Express* (London), *Daily Telegraph* (London)

Reviews: Walter Kerr (*New York Herald Tribune*), Howard Taubman (*New York Times*), Brooks Atkinson (*New York Times*), Edwin Denby (*New York Herald Tribune*), Virgil Thomson (*New York Herald Tribune*), Kenneth Tynan (*The New Yorker*), Wolcott Gibbs (*The New Yorker*), Martin Gottfried (*Women's Wear Daily*), Leo Lerman (*Dance Magazine*), Robert Coleman (*Daily Mirror*), William Hawkins (*New York World Telegram*), Jack Gould (*New York Times*), John Crosby (*New York Herald Tribune*), Irene Thirer (*New York Herald Tribune*), Elliot Norton (*Boston Daily Record, Boston Post*), Cecil Smith (*Chicago Daily Tribune*), Claudia Cassidy (*Chicago Journal of Commerce*), Alfred Frankenstein (*San Francisco Chronicle*), Henry Gilford (*Dance Observer*), Arthur Weiler (*New York Times*), Edwin P. Melvin (*Christian Science Monitor*), Elinor Hughes (*Boston Herald*), Cyrus Durgin (*Boston Daily Globe*), Harriett Johnson (*New York Post*), Ann Barzel (*Dance Magazine*), George Beiswanger (*Theatre Arts Monthly*, April 1939)

Interviews and letters: Mary Wigman, Valerie Bettis, Louise Kloepper, Glen Tetley, Mary Anthony, Marva Spelman, Elizabeth Harris, Doris Rudko, Thelma Cowan

Index